Papa

A Personal Memoir

Papa

A Personal Memoir

Gregory H. Hemingway, M.D.

with a Preface by Norman Mailer

BOSTON 1976
HOUGHTON MIFFLIN COMPANY

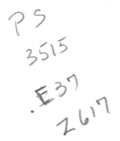

Copyright© 1976 by Gregory H. Hemingway
Preface copyright © 1976 by Norman Mailer

Library of Congress Cataloging in Publication Data
Hemingway, Gregory, date
Papa: a personal memoir.
1. Hemingway, Ernest, 1899–1961—Biography.
I. Title.
PS3515.E37Z617   813'.5'2 [B]   76-6933
ISBN 0-395-24348-3

Printed in the United States of America

v 10 9 8 7 6 5 4 3 2 1

This book is for
Ted Hager and Mr. Bud Parr

The smallest boy was fair and was built like a pocket battle-ship. He was a copy of Thomas Hudson, physically, reduced in scale and widened and shortened. His skin freckled when it tanned and he had a humorous face and was born being very old. He was a devil too, and deviled both his older brothers, and he had a dark side to him that nobody except Thomas Hudson could ever understand. Neither of them thought about this except that they recognized it in each other and knew it was bad and the man respected it and understood the boy's having it. They were very close to each other although Thomas Hudson had never been as much with this boy as with the others. This youngest boy, Andrew, was a precocious excellent athlete and he had been marvelous with horses since he had first ridden. The other boys were very proud of him but they did not want any nonsense from him, either. He was a little unbelievable and anyone could well have doubted his feats except that many people had seen him ride and watched him jump and seen his cold, professional modesty. He was a boy born to be quite wicked who was being very good and he carried his wickedness around with him transmuted into a sort of teasing gaiety. But he was a bad boy and the others knew it and he knew it. He was just being good while his badness grew inside him.

— Ernest Hemingway, from *Islands in the Stream*

THE AUTHOR wishes to acknowledge the research, editorial assistance, and general encouragement of the following people: Denis Brian, Helen Darval, Ralph Fuentes, Valerie Hemingway, Deidre Maguire, J. Simon Prager, Stan Weissburg and, especially, Bill Weatherby.

Preface

Whateriterize every book about Hemingway I have read is the way his character remains out of focus. Even a writer with an edge as hard as Lillian Ross did not seem able to catch him properly in her famous *New Yorker* piece. Hemingway was there, but much too precise in his portrait as if he had sat for one of those neo-realistic paintings where the pride of the artist is to make the subject look as if he has been photographed, not painted.

For contrast, there is Carlos Baker's monumental biography and it gives us an immense amount of day-to-day material somewhat modestly undigested. It is nonetheless an invaluable book which every ambitious biography to come will evaluate detail by detail, a necessary task, for Baker's book was written with a determinedly soft focus as if the author felt his literary mission was not so much to present the man as to cover every year of Hemingway's existence in the recollections of his friends.

There is also A. E. Hotchner's book which gives a portrait, and most readable it is, but askew. Hotchner is using a wide-angle

lens; the very nostrils of the great man are distorted. Sadly we
learn there is reason to believe the materials are transposed. A
long and marvelously articulated speech which Hemingway
makes once to Hotchner turns out in fact to have been taken from
a letter. It is a minor literary peccadillo of the sort professional
magazine writers commit often, since their skills mature in a
school which demands you tell your story fast and make it track
(and a quotation from a letter comes off slower than a man
talking), but such methods breed distortion with their speed.

Now, we have here a book written by a son about his father,
written by a son who is not a professional writer as he is quick to
tell you (although he can write interestingly enough — it may
even be a book which will be read at one sitting by more than
half the readers who pick it up). That is because it is unlike most
books written by sons about great fathers. There is nothing
slavish here. The son lies to the father, and the father pays him
back, meanly; the son loves the father and the father loves him
back, but in his own style, and it is remote enough for the son to
hate him a little as well. If it is a portrait written in love, it is with
all the sweets and sours of love. What characterizes love when
not wholly blissful is how damnably sweet and sour it gets. It
kills any man or woman if they have the bad luck to be deeply in
love with a veritable son of a bitch, and every bad thing we have
ever heard about Hemingway can find its echo in this book. You
do not have to wonder when you are done why any number of
men and women could know Hemingway well and hate him.
Yet everything fine, noble, attractive, and splendid in the man
comes in with its echo as well. For once, you can read a book
about Hemingway and not have to decide whether you like him
or not. He is there. By God, he exists. He is a father, good and

bad by turns, even sensational and godawful on different days of the year, and his contradictions are now his unity, his dirty fighting and his love of craft come out of the same blood. We can feel the man present before us, and his complexes have now become no more than his moods. His pride and his evasions have become one man, his innocence and sophistication, his honesty and outsize snobbery, his romantic madness and inconceivably practical sense of how to be outrageously romantic, it all comes through as in no other book about Hemingway, and for the simplest reason — the father was real to the son. Whereas those of us who approach Hemingway from without have been in the position of trying to find the reality behind the legend, and that is an especially contemporary form of analysis which tends to come out wrong. Hemingway, when all is said, was a Midwestern boy seized by success and ripped out of every root, and he spent the rest of his life in trying to relocate some of his old sense of terra firma by following each movement of the wind (and there were many) through his talent and his dread. What a remarkable achievement, that the sense of that talent and dread, while hardly ever referred to in these pages, is nonetheless in every paragraph of this unassuming and affective memoir.

— NORMAN MAILER

Contents

Papa

A Personal Memoir

Death Be Not Proud

I NEVER GOT OVER a sense of responsibility for my father's death and the recollection of it sometimes made me act in strange ways. In 1966, five years after he killed himself, I went to a cocktail party in Miami for some newspapermen who were covering the Candy Mossler trial. The party was a large one, hosted by a friend of mine, a staff member of the Miami *Herald*. Guests drifted around the house, drinks in hand, discussing the trial.

One of the reporters was a pleasant-faced man in his twenties, a big fellow over six-feet-two and weighing about 220 pounds. He immediately made the connection with my last name, and asked me some innocuous questions about my father. Such questions always bored and sometimes irritated me, but I was used to them by then, and I politely gave him the stock answers reserved for such occasions.

That seemed to be that, but then I saw him again about half an hour later, sitting on a couch with his head in his hands, crying. It's disturbing to see a grown man, especially a young, vigorous one, crying, so I put my hand on his shoulder and said, "John, is there anything I can do?"

"I think it's awful what happened to Ernest Hemingway," he said, staring straight into my eyes, too intently for comfort.

I couldn't have agreed with him more.

But a kaleidoscope of emotions went through me. You can't keep mulling over the past, it can hurt you, you have to extricate yourself from the memory of some things — this guy must be crazy to get emotionally involved with someone he had never met. Hemingway was my father, not just a person in the public domain, and his death was a shock to me. Doesn't this fool realize I have some very strong feelings on the subject?

Then a feeling of disgust overwhelmed me and I thought, oh well, fuck him. I said, "If you feel so strongly about it then why don't you go out to Idaho and tend his grave." And I walked away from him.

A few minutes later, as I was talking to someone else, he hit me from the blind side and sent me hurtling across the room. Little multicolored lights flashed in my brain, the sensation you get when the retina is stimulated by pressure. I don't remember much else until they pulled me off him. I had broken his nose, knocked out two of his front teeth, and half of one of his ears was hanging loosely from the side of his head. He was aspirating so much blood that I was afraid he might choke to death. I turned him over, face down, and, with some help, dragged him out on the porch.

The host (whose four small children were asleep during the party) discovered that somebody had turned on all four gas jets in the kitchen without lighting the stove. I assumed it was this same guy. We got in touch with his wife and managed to put him in the back seat of their car. He was breathing, but was still unconscious.

Oddly enough, the next morning, after my head had cleared, I couldn't feel any pity for him or any shame for what I had done — and this is the frightening thing — I felt good, almost elated. I found myself thinking, "Damn, I might have been able to take papa on the best day he ever had!"

But I never would have tried.

In his youth, my father was not a bully, a sick bore, or a professional celebrity. In later life, in drunken revels with syco-phants, revels which merely anaesthetized the pain which had accompanied the loss of his talent, the man I had known would never have left a record that provided a permanent feast off a carcass the literary vultures thought they had already picked clean.

The man I remembered was kind, gentle, elemental in his vastness, tormented beyond endurance, and although we always called him papa, it was out of love, not fear.

The man I knew in my youth was quite a man, not A. E. Hotchner's *Papa Hemingway*.

I'll tell you about him.

He used to say that he imagined how a sentence sounded in his mind before he wrote it down. He would try it all different ways and one way would "sound best." When the people were talking, he said, it came out so fast that sometimes he couldn't keep up with it on the typewriter. That's why I couldn't under-stand in the late forties and fifties when he would write to critics such as Carlos Baker and Malcolm Cowley that "writing is a métier triste" and "it's a 'hard trade,' " and other similar self-pitying things.

Now I know he simply meant that the material wasn't flowing out naturally anymore — the well was no longer artesian but needed pumping. He always had the marvelous ear for words and he was certainly more experienced and wiser, but the old effortless elemental naturalness was no longer there. The world no longer flowed through him as through a purifying filter, with the distillate seeming more true and beautiful than the world itself. He was no longer a poet, one of God's spies, but a querulous counterespionage agent whose operatives seemed to deceive him.

The single exception was a short period when the platonic affair with a young Italian noblewoman who visited his Cuban farm somehow got his creative juices flowing again. *The Old Man and the Sea* came out of that period, along with the first and third parts of a lesser unfinished work, *Islands in the Stream*. The humility and empathy for man's fate, which the Nobel Prize Committee remarked on and which it interpreted as "growth," was the result of his seeing what it was "truly" like to be without his genius — and the knowledge of what it was like for the rest of the people all of the time to be uncushioned from the world by the intellectual and material rewards of genius.

He always tried hard to win and hated to lose and used to say, "You make your own luck, Gig," and "You know what makes a good loser? Practice." Maybe he learned during the drought of his talent that what makes a loser, good or bad, is fate.

He had always had everything. Handsome as a movie star in

his youth, with an attraction for women you wouldn't believe unless you saw it; extremely sensitive, blessed with a constitution, energy, and resiliency that allowed him to abuse his body and recover from trauma, both physical and emotional, that destroyed lesser men; supremely imaginative and yet possessed of tremendous common sense, perhaps the rarest combination of qualities; and luck, almost always good, the genetic good luck to have all of the above, and the luck to survive a major war wound with the knowledge of what the edge of nothingness is like.

Is there any wonder that such a man became rancorous and short-tempered when his talent began to ebb after the publication of *For Whom the Bell Tolls*? While you still have all those gifts, plus the ability to describe what they enable you to understand, you can't be a megalomaniac, but when that talent leaves you it is understandable that you could.

And then, like an Indian Summer, the talent returns and you produce a short masterpiece (there is no time in an Indian Summer for a long one) so full of love and empathy and understanding. And then the long Fall and last Bitter Winter sets in for good.

When you knew my father for a long time in his youth you could only love him and marvel at him, and when you knew him when he got older you could only be sad or bitter — depending on how well you had known him when he was young.

He never could develop a philosophy that would allow him to grow old gracefully, but if I had had all his talent and experience, and could imagine as profoundly as he could what awaits us all, maybe I couldn't either. I have seen that look on a wounded animal's face that seems to say, "Shoot me, I'm in pain." But man is the only animal that can pull the trigger, and many men helped my father pull it.

In 1951, when my father was fifty-two and I was nineteen, I got into some trouble on the West Coast for taking a mind-stimulating drug before such things had become fashionable. My mother, who was visiting her sister Jinny in San Francisco, did not seem at all alarmed by my predicament but thought my father should be notified.

When I said that it would be simpler if papa were not brought in she said, yes . . . a lot of things would be simpler if you had only one parent. But she wasn't really at all upset. I can remember this as clearly as if it were yesterday. She was thin and a little haggard looking and intermittently endured severe headaches. But she had been having those for several months and we weren't too alarmed because she said she was going to the Mayo Clinic soon for a complete checkup: "From head to toe, Gig," was the way she put it.

She put in a long distance call to papa in Cuba to tell him what had happened. My aunt, who hated my father's guts and who certainly couldn't be considered an unbiased witness, said the conversation had started out calmly enough. But soon Mother was shouting into the phone and sobbing uncontrollably.

I'd seen papa's ability for destroying people with words, and had even seen him use it on Mother. Once he had written her a letter entitled, "How Green Was My Valet," with Mother portrayed as Hettie Green, the eccentric Wall Street millionairess, and the "valet" referring to the nature of their former relationship.

But Aunt Jinny told me nothing of the details of the phone conversation the next morning, just that Mother was dead. She had finished talking with my father around nine p.m., had gone to bed soon afterward, and had awakened around one a.m. with a severe abdominal pain. The pain had become worse and she was rushed to the hospital, where she died on the operating table three hours later.

What happened next is still a little hazy. If you've ever seen the movie of Françoise Sagan's *Bonjour Tristesse,* you may remember that the heroine causes the automobile accident that claims the life of her father's new wife. To show how her outlook on everything has changed, the director shoots the rest of the film through a yellow and green filter in blurred focus.

That is sort of the way it was with me. Everything changed. My mother's face looked unbelievably white at the funeral, and I remember thinking through sobs what a barbarous ritual Anglo-Saxon burial is.

But time tends to heal, to put things in proper perspective, and I got a little better. Besides, from being a poor aircraft mechanic struggling to support a wife and child, I was suddenly a rich young man, having inherited a small fortune from my mother. I'd been left exactly the same amount as my brother, which surprised me because I had always been sure that she loved him more. But I realized she had loved me more than I had thought.

But somehow it was wrong. The things that I had wanted before weren't fun now that I could afford them. I wasn't sure why.

A few months after the funeral, with an advance on my inheritance from Mother's attorney financing the journey, I took my wife, Jane, and our young daughter, Lorian, down to Cuba to my father's house, the Finca. He hadn't seen my wife before and was pleased with my choice: she was a bright girl and beautiful, having been a Powers model before we were married. Jane was part Indian, perhaps an eighth, and had those high cheekbones that photographers and my father loved. Perhaps she reminded him of the Indian girl he'd had in his youth. I don't really know; we didn't discuss it.

Toward the end of the visit I began to feel pretty good. It was fun doing again all the things that I'd loved so much in my earlier years, and introducing them to Jane.

Then, one afternoon, feeling in an expansive mood, I talked with my father about my future plans and all that had happened recently. Referring to the trouble I'd gotten into on the Coast, I said, "It wasn't so bad, really, papa."

"No? Well, it killed Mother." Whatever his motives were, the yellow-green filter came back down over my eyes and this time it didn't go away for seven years. I didn't say anything back to him. He'd almost always been right about things, he was so sound, I knew he loved me, it must have been something he just had to say, and I believed him.

When we left the Finca for the airport I remember papa remarking, "Well, don't take any wooden trust funds." I could see the humor and I smiled as we were parting.

I never saw my father again because of course the coffin was closed at *his* funeral.

My wife persuaded me to study medicine. Your grandfather was a doctor, she said, and you can be a good one too. Thank you, Jane. When papa crashed in Africa in 1954, I was in my

second year of pre-med at U.C.L.A. The first headlines announced that the wreckage of the plane had been sighted and
that there was no sign of life. Thinking he was dead, I realized
how much I still loved him. When I found out soon afterward
that he had survived, I resolved to patch up our differences.

After he won the Nobel Prize that October, I sent him a
congratulatory wire. He replied immediately, enclosing a
check for $5000, which he said was right off the top of the tax-
free bounty of Sweden. Moved by his generosity, I decided to
take a trip to Africa. Though I'd done fairly well in my pre-med
courses, earning a B+ average, I knew that I didn't then have
the mental stability to be a doctor, knew that my mind was
shot, at least temporarily. I didn't even apply to medical
school.

I'd been brought up on the romance of Africa. The "real"
thing for me was not the Martin Johnson movies of "dis-
covering" the dark continent, with natives in ostrich-plume
headdresses surrounding his zebra-striped plane, but the
stuffed animal heads that graced the walls of the house where I
had grown up in Key West, the lion rug on the floor, and *Green
Hills of Africa,* that beautiful book describing my parents' safari.
I wanted to see those green hills. Perhaps there was solace in
them.

I was fascinated with elephants too. Perhaps if I'd been more
of a seafaring man I'd have taken to the point and been a har-
pooner, going after the greatest creature of them all. But no
white whales, please, no white elephants; the thing I was hunting was huge, but blacker in my mind.

I would pick up elephant tracks at dawn, following my
tracker through the heat of the day, never stopping unless I

lost the track, never taking a sip of water until I was sure of the outcome of the pursuit. And finally we would catch up with them around four, usually under some giant tree, where they, with their four-hour head start, had stopped to wait out the heat of the day under an acacia tree. The danger — and the excitement — increased, the closer you got to them. And then the shot: the heart was surer, but the brain, though slightly more difficult, was quicker, and after a while I always took the brain.

Then the terrible sadness when I saw this great creature lifeless on the ground and realized that he would never again play with his family, in an almost human way, would no longer reach for succulent branches that no other animal even thought of trying to reach, would no longer make sounds like God's thunder when digesting his meals.

But my remorse over the elephant's death would quickly pass — I was almost as tired as they by four p.m. and would often sleep while my trackers cut and chopped the valuable tusks out of the skulls. The tusks were sold to Indian smugglers for an anaesthetic — alcohol — and supplies for more hunts. My trackers must have thought I was becoming a wealthy man. But I already was wealthy, in a sense. The hunt, you see, was the thing, an end in itself.

I shot eighteen elephants one month, God save my soul. But it's no use running when you're sick, because when you finally stop, you find you're just as sick as when you started. When people ask me if I ever hunted with my father, I say no, but with a peculiar smile, because of course he's been with me on many an African hunt. Africa was no refuge. I worked three years as an apprentice professional hunter. I learned Swahili, how to fix Land-Rovers, and where the animals were and how to shoot them. But I hadn't learned how to control my drinking while I was in town, and as that was the only time the game department officials saw me, I never got my professional hunter's license. They thought I was too unstable, and they were right.

I felt guilty about Mother's inheritance, thought that since I had killed her it was blood money, and I got rid of it incredibly fast. My marriage finally broke up and I was drafted into the army. I volunteered for the paratroops but washed out when I couldn't make the five-mile run. (Who knows, I might also have been afraid to jump out of airplanes.) After an undistinguished career in the peacetime army, I went back to Africa to do more killing. Somehow it was therapeutic. Although the yellow-green emotional filter was still in place, the focus of my mind was sharpening.

I returned to the United States to finish my last year of pre-med and start medical school. One of the first things I did was to write the hospital where Mother had died and ask them for an autopsy report. When it came, it showed that she had died of pheochromocytoma, which is a rare and unusual tumor of the adrenal gland.

It is unusual because the tumor does not kill by invading vital organs, but by secreting abnormally large amounts of adrenaline — which then make the blood pressure rise to incredible heights, often causing a rupture of an artery. There are two varieties of the tumor, the intermittent and the constantly secreting types. Judging from the symptoms prior to her death, I would guess that my mother's had been the intermittent variety.

A stimulus as slight as standing up suddenly, being bumped from behind in a crowd, or getting emotionally upset by a bad dream could make the intermittent type "fire off" and start putting out those tremendous quantities of adrenaline. The irony was that the Mayo Clinic, where my mother had intended to go in a few weeks for a checkup, was one of the two or three institutions in the United States at that time where there was a decent chance of successfully removing such a tumor.

I wrote my father all this in the summer of 1960, pointing out that it was not my minor troubles that had upset Mother but his brutal phone conversation with her eight hours before she died. The tumor had become necrotic or rotten and when it fired off that night, it sent her blood pressure skyrocketing; a medium-sized blood vessel, within or adjacent to the rotten area, had ruptured. Then the tumor stopped discharging adrenaline, her blood pressure dropped from about 300 to 0, and she died of shock on the operating table.

I can imagine the wild frustration of the surgeons as they searched for a bleeding point in the abdomen, where Mother had originally felt the pain, to account for this fatal drop in blood pressure. The operative report showed they found no blood in the abdominal cavity and the autopsy showed only 500 cc. of blood in the space around her right kidney.

My father, a doctor's son and a man who had a considerable knowledge of medicine, must have imagined the surgeons' frenzy, too. According to a person who was with him in Havana when he received my letter, he raged at first and then walked around the house in silence for the rest of the day.

About three months later his first noticeable symptoms of paranoia began, with the worries about the FBI chasing him for income tax evasion. Or was it the great FIB, finally coming home to roost?

I hope that this whole seemingly fatal time sequence was coincidental. I had become wary of thinking that because one event closely precedes another it is in fact its true cause. God knows, I would never have written my father if I had thought it would upset him as much as it did. There's a tremendous difference between wanting to kill someone in your unconscious and actually committing the deed. It is a difference that makes us human.

Besides, one who could dish it out, as he could, surely must be prepared to take it. Hadn't we always told each other the truth?

My father called me when I wrote him I had been accepted into the University of Miami medical school. It was the usual lousy connection from Cuba. His voice was strangely mirthless, repeating the instructions over and over to the operator until we finally got through.

"Congratulations, Gig. But I doubt if you'll ever make much of a doctor — you can't even spell the word medicine correctly."

I laughed because I had finally got started in something worthwhile and I knew he was proud of me in spite of his rough joking.

But he went on in the same monotone. "Your grandfather was a good doctor but he killed himself. (Pause.) I saw a good doctor today who told me I had a rare disease that makes you blind and permanently impotent."

It took a few seconds for his words to sink. But I often wonder if I ever really did understand what they must have meant to him. I can still hear that flat bitter tone in his voice.

I said the usual things — Cuban doctors aren't worth a

damn, go to New York, get another opinion. Apologies: most Cuban doctors are adequate and some are excellent.

"I don't know anybody up there," I said, "but I know people who do and I'll make some calls."

"I've already made the calls — I'm going up soon. It's only a matter of time."

Then his voice changed for a moment. "Remember that painting by Bosch of the end of the world? All the devils were rounding up the sinners and I pointed out one man robed like a gentleman who was rising from his table indignantly and drawing his sword. Remember? I pointed him out to you, out of all those grotesque figures, and said, see, see him there, he thinks he can handle death with a sword? And you seemed to understand so well what I was saying."

According to people who were near him, he was a completely changed man after that visit to the doctor. He never went out anymore, there was no more gaiety, no more good times at the Finca. It was as if he had already given up living.

It didn't matter that there is no common medical condition besides diabetes mellitus, which he didn't have, that causes both impotence and blindness. And when you consult an eye doctor, the ophthalmologist doesn't volunteer that your eye condition is part of a syndrome that is going to make you impotent as well.

Reconstructing what probably happened, I suspect that papa must have asked whether his eye condition could cause impotence and the doctor, unthinkingly, said, well, yes, it *could*, the way doctors sometimes equivocate when they don't know what they're talking about. Papa had probably been worrying about his failing sexual prowess for some time. Remember, impotence means different things to different people. For some, not being able to perform as they could ten years earlier is a dread sign that their sexually active days are numbered.

The psychiatrists tell us that 95 percent of all cases of impotence have a psychological basis. Probably. But God knows, papa had enough possible physical causes, too. His liver had been in poor shape for years. Even in the male, the adrenal glands produce estrogen, or female hormones, which are normally broken down in the liver. But if the liver is badly damaged, there can be a high concentration of estrogen in the bloodstream which will reduce the male libido.

But perhaps the worst offender was reserpine, the drug he was taking in large doses to control his blood pressure. This can not only cause mental depression, but has a specific paralytic effect on the parasympathetic nerves that control the sexual mechanism. Moreover, the depressive effects of reserpine can last for months after the drug is discontinued, a fact that may not have been known at the time my father was being treated in 1961.

Poor old papa. It made little difference that he got a different and more expert opinion about his eyes when he went to the New York specialist. It didn't matter that the really topnotch Park Avenue man told him there was nothing seriously wrong with them. He knew he couldn't see well even after he got the new lens the great specialist had prescribed. And he probably didn't even ask the specialist about the impotence thing. One medical opinion on that painful subject, since it confirmed his own diagnosis, was enough. He was so deep in depression by then that he probably wouldn't have believed the doctor anyway. He'd seen his own father try to cheer up hopeless cases years before.

It seems almost appropriate that some people should grow

old and feeble, as their advanced age has finally given their original weakness dignity and made them whole. But my father was never feeble in any way in his youth, either intellectually or physically, and when he became so he refused to accept it. I think he showed courage in accepting the only option left.

Key West

I WAS THE THIRD and youngest son, the product of one of my father's cumulative emotional catastrophes. That is, one of his four marriages. My mother, Pauline, was his second wife; she had wooed him away from his first, Hadley, when he was writing *The Sun Also Rises*. Papa and Hadley had one son, Jack.

I was born in 1931; Patrick, my full brother, was three and a half years older, and we were both born by Caesarean section. In the thirties, doctors thought that more than two Caesareans would cause a woman's uterus to rupture, and my mother was told not to have any more children. My father had wanted a daughter badly, so to my mother my birth meant that she, or perhaps I, had blown this last chance to make her lovable egomaniac happy. Patrick, on the other hand, had been born during the first few eruptions of her volcanic affair with papa. She loved Pat very much and showed it, which is certainly no crime, but unfortunately was so construed by me.

I must have tried just about everything to get Mother's attention, but I might as well have been a burr under a horse's saddle. I tried imitating Pat, but that didn't work. I imitated papa, but with even less success. That really surprised me. Christ. I knew how much Mother loved papa.

Once, after their divorce, when she was fondly admiring a photo of papa as a boy, I suggested that I looked just the least bit like him, maybe?

"You don't look at all alike," she said in a flat, matter-of-fact voice. "There's just a superficial resemblance because both of you have your hair cut in bangs."

And then, almost in a whisper, as if thinking out loud, not meaning to hurt: "God, he was handsome then, look at those *eyes*, so alive and interested."

Mother left my rearing entirely to Ada, an odd sort of Prussian governess, who had never married in her youth, which by the time we met was far behind her.

When I was an infant, there was a theory that you should ignore a baby when he cried for the bottle, as crying would develop his lungs. I am told Ada adhered to this method religiously.

My parents would often go off on long jaunts somewhere, leaving me with Ada. I was about three and a half when they took the nine-month safari that produced *Green Hills of Africa*, and I was sent north with Ada to her home in Syracuse, New York; a more pleasant boarding arrangement had been made for Patrick.

Any infraction of her innumerable rules would cause her to fly into a screaming fit and start eating the carpet, as the Germans say. She would pack her bags and go hobbling down the stairs with me clinging to her skirts, screaming, "Ada, don't leave me, please don't leave me!"

"All right, I'll stay, you little shitsky. But if you misbehave one more time . . ." We played it as a serious scene for years, and until I realized one day that she was only kidding, she had me where she wanted me.

My mother made her absences in the early and most formative years of my life readily explicable later on, when she admitted, "Gig, I just don't have much of what's called a maternal instinct, I guess. I can't *stand* horrid little children until they are five or six — they're still pretty awful then, but at least I can communicate with them on a semi-rational level. That is why Ada always took care of you. But I loved you, darling, I really did, though I guess I didn't always show it." Understood completely and forgiven. But not originally.

Are you beginning to see why I formed what psychiatrists call a "dangerously" close relationship with my father?

Oddly enough, however, my first memory of papa is of him shouting at me. It was early morning and I was playing on our lawn in Key West, banging a couple of pans together and making a hell of a racket. Suddenly he loomed above me on the second-floor porch, looking enormous and angry, and shouted down, "Will you *please be quiet!* I'm trying to write." He never yelled at me again.

Other memories of Key West return in flashes, incomplete. The old Spanish-style house that we lived in was two stories high, with porches running around both levels; it had high ceilings and was considered much cooler than other houses on the island. Mother was always fixing and changing and remodeling. She even put in a swimming pool, the only one between Miami and Panama, she said proudly. But by the time it was finished, so was our family.

Although my early childhood coincided with the Depression, our family had few financial problems. This was partly due to papa's royalties from *The Sun Also Rises* and *A Farewell to Arms,* but mainly because my mother was rich, a Sloan's liniment or pain-in-the-ass heiress, as I sometimes thought of her. While Mother's money made us secure, a high wall around the one-acre property shielded us from some of the harsher realities. But almost every day derelicts would come to the gate and say, "Sonny, can I have a dime for a can of beans so I can go up on the Keys?" What a noble and romantic thing to do, I thought! It was like setting out on the open road, with all your worldly goods in a red bandanna tied to the end of a stick.

But one day I followed one of these poor bums after giving him the dime, wondering how a pittance could finance such a great journey. I followed him all the way up Whitehead Street, almost to the end of the island, and was getting tired and about to turn back when he went into Sloppy Joe's and bought a beer.

I wish I could remember more about Mr. Josie's bar because, according to people who have written about my father, some very interesting conversations took place there. And interesting meetings too, like the first between my father and the woman who replaced my mother, his third wife, Martha Gellhorn. But I wasn't allowed in most of the time, being too young, and I had to wait in the rumble seat of the car, while papa had a "quick one." But sometimes Mr. Josie and papa would let me come in, if the place wasn't crowded.

The bar itself was very long with tall slender stools on one side; behind it was a picture of Custer's Last Stand. This was the famous lithograph which showed Long Hair, a look of confidence and arrogance on his face, surrounded by lots of pale, dead Indians, but with many more very red, live Indians pressing in for the kill. "Giving them hell, ain't he, kid?" an old rummy said when he first saw me mesmerized by the picture.

Down at the far corner of the bar, another rummy, a one-legged one, could usually be found sitting on the floor. He'd said, "Come here, kid. Give an old vet a hand." But when I went to see what I could do for him he tried to hit me with his crutch. I never approached that old bastard again.

Then there was Willy Gates, a third baseman of local renown who once had tried out with the Brooklyn Dodgers, but who had lost his arm — not literally, of course, like the rummy's leg. He always seemed sad and just sat there, thinking about that great arm, I suppose, and occasionally anaesthetizing the memory of his loss. And I loved Skinner, the giant black handyman, with his Louis Armstrong smile, who could always cadge a drink by squatting under the piano and lifting it off the floor for a few seconds on his massive shoulders. Sloppy Joe's was exciting when they'd let me in.

But tagging along with papa when he was in town wasn't always easy. He loved to fish and it seemed as if he was out on the water every day. I loved the sea, and the fishing was beautiful too. The sailfish would come out of the water in the most unexpected places, leaping high in the air, as graceful as Nureyev, and falling flat on their side, the way I'm sure Nureyev would like to fall if he were in the sea.

But I'd usually miss all that because I'd be downstairs in the head vomiting, or rolling on my bunk in the deathless agony that only seasick people really know. Once I went below, it would be for the rest of the day, because the gasoline fumes were more concentrated down there, compounding my illness. But I was determined to be with my father and never missed a trip. "Glad to have you aboard again, Mr. Gig," he'd say with a smile.

The fish would look great, too, when we brought them home and hung them up on the dock all in rows, the green and yellow hues gone in death from the dolphin, but the wahoo, the real greyhound of the seas, still sleek and beautiful, looking capable again of taking all the line off your reel in one incredible run. People would mill around to see what we had caught, asking the names of the fish, and papa invariably answered their questions politely and patiently.

And at least I'd be on that wonderful, solid dock.

You could catch just about anything off Key West, and for a while papa held the Atlantic record for sailfish caught on rod and reel, 119 pounds. More fish stories later, but not too many, I promise.

Memories, pictures flash and disappear before I can identify them.

I remember playing wonderful war games with papa on the lawn when he came home from Spain in 1937. He had brought back firecrackers, so we had imaginary armies moving into battle against each other, complete with cannon fire and puffs of smoke. God, how I wanted to go back to Spain with him when he left.

Another time he brought back some peacocks, and watching the males spread their tails and do their courting dance for hens was a lovely introduction to the mysteries of sex. I remember, too, showing him *Ferdinand the Bull*, which I rather liked then. "That goddamn kids' book has made ten times more than

Death in the Afternoon," he said. "I worked harder on *Death in the Afternoon* than on any book in my life, and that jerk who wrote *Ferdinand* might have spent a month on it."

Mr. Sinclair Lewis came to the house, perhaps to commiserate with papa about Ferdinand. He scared the hell out of us kids, with his face like a death's head, all blotchy and red. Maybe he saw the horrified expression I couldn't suppress at our introduction, because he didn't stay too long.

My parents were divorced in 1940. Mother got custody of Patrick and me, along with some "punitive" alimony because papa had been the guilty party. I can't remember much of the divorce period, just shouting in other rooms, doors slamming, Mother scurrying out of their bedroom crying — the usual "amicable" divorce.

This was all part of the adult world, and although things were obviously not going well in that world, I felt strangely detached from it. Once the internecine war had ended, the only permanent change was that papa didn't live with us anymore. Instead of seeing him for brief interludes between his travels to Africa, Spain, and China, I was to be with him every summer, the whole goddamn summer, without Mother or Ada, wherever papa might be, in Bimini, Sun Valley, or Havana. It was really better that way.

Bimini

IN THE THIRTIES, before my parents were divorced, we sometimes spent the spring and early summer in Bimini, a narrow
Bahamian island forty-seven miles east of Miami. Bimini lies
on the eastern border of the Gulf Stream, and from its highest
point, looking toward Miami and the fat, flat Dadeland to the
west, you can see nearly halfway to a famous beach renowned
for its aged women wrapped in mink to ward off the air-condi-
tioned chill and tottering on imitation-gold spiked heels.
Thank God the world is round or we could have seen it all from
there.

The color of Bimini's water changes within two hundred
yards of the shore from shimmeringly clear white near the fine
sandy beach, to green, to aquamarine, and finally to the time-
less deep blue of the Gulf Stream. My father thought of that
stream as a great river, thirty miles wide and six hundred fathoms deep, extending from the Sargasso Sea to England, and
bringing warmth and sustenance to whatever it touched. He
wrote that scows from Havana could dump tons of garbage in
it daily and there wouldn't be a trace five miles downstream.

But even the sea can endure only so much. Recently, I'm reliably informed, a two-hundred-pound piece of shit was boated off Bimini, a record for rod and reel.

Whenever I see the stream now I think of what he wrote and I try to remember it and him as they were when I was young in Bimini.

Our whole family — Mother, my brothers Jack and Pat, who were then fourteen and nine, myself, and my nurse Ada — would make the trip over on papa's cabin cruiser the *Pilar*. The *Pilar* was about forty feet long, painted black, and had been "built to papa's specifications," which I soon learned meant "built for fishing, not pleasure boating." The translation for that, I later learned, was that he had run out of money after ordering the best engines and fighting chair available and there had been none left over to make the boat comfortable.

Once we arrived, papa kept the *Pilar* moored to the dock of the Compleat Angler Hotel when he wasn't out fishing. Mrs. Duncomb, the proprietress, a lively, delightful octogenarian survivor of old colonial England — fishing, anyone? — kept an excellent table.

"Go wherever you want, kids. There's plenty of Bimini to explore and you can't get lost here," papa told us one morning, making it clear that only adults would be going out on the boat that day.

We took off along the great course of deserted beach to the north, gathering shells, skipping flat rocks on the clear water, and stopping to build castles more elaborate than crusaders had ever ravaged in their dreams.

"What fish can you get tomorrow?" Pat asked, looking far out toward the blue water.

"Anything," Jack replied. "It's late in May so they'll have the big baits rigged for giant tuna, but we'll be trolling a feather, too, and this time of year on that feather we can catch amber-jack, bonito, Allison tuna, barracuda, grouper, mackerel, wahoo — "

Then, Pat said softly, "I hope they won't make me sit in the fighting chair."

"No chance, little brother. After the way you let go of the whole rig and lost five hundred dollars' worth of tackle last year, they won't let you near the chair."

Pat didn't answer back. He would probably never forget the time the adults had let him sit in the fighting chair while they had lunch, and how a marlin had hit the feather while he was holding the rod. The force of the strike was so great that it would have jerked him overboard if he'd tried to hold the rod. Instinctively he had sensed the strength of the fish, and had just let go, relinquishing rod, reel, and line to the sea.

"Jesus Christ, you lost the whole goddamn rig," papa yelled.

Mother was quick, too.

"For God's sake, what else could he have done, Ernest?"

Papa had simply been reacting to his loss, and must have realized that even before he finished speaking. He began to make light of the whole thing and emphasized over and over again that Patrick had no other choice. But the damage had been done. In Patrick's mind, fishing had become, for the fore-seeable future, an adult sport.

"I don't have to go out tomorrow, do I, Jack?" I said, as we continued up the beach. He smiled kindly, remembering how I always got seasick on the *Pilar*.

"It might be calm, Gig."

"Okay, I'll go."

"Maybe papa will let *me* sit in the fighting chair," Jack said. "I'm almost fifteen."

"Maybe," Pat said.

Despite our fantasies, fishing from the *Pilar* was almost entirely for the adults. But we remained keen observers. It was Mike Lerner, owner of a chain of women's wear shops, who had taught papa how to fish for tuna. Papa would often tell about the advice Mike gave him:

"Ernest, you have to bring these fish up fast. After they're hooked they make one long sounding run, go almost straight down, and die down there from the pressure of the depth. Then you have to bring up anywhere from four to eight hundred pounds of dead weight from at least fifteen hundred feet — and you have to do it before the sharks get the blood scent. But there are just too many sharks here. Once the first shark finds and bites your fish there's so much blood that ten others show up in a flash, tearing at the meat and shaking their heads to get great chunks free. By the time you get the tuna to the surface he's just a tail, stripped bones, and a head. No one has ever landed an unmutilated tuna here."

That night, down at one of the bars, Bill Leeds, an experienced drinker and fisherman, asked papa what everyone had been talking about since our arrival.

"Do you think you can bring in a whole one, Ernest?"

"I doubt it, Bill. But we'll give it a try. Tomorrow."

Next morning we dressed early and were ready for breakfast before dawn. Papa wanted to be clear of the harbor by the time the sun came up.

The wind had started blowing during the night and the ocean

was flecked with whitecaps as we headed out through the surf toward the Gulf Stream. We couldn't see the water change color as we pounded into the waves; it was all just a dirty slate gray.

The *Pilar* had no flying bridge then, and we couldn't go up top to get away from the gas fumes. With the smell of the gas and the constant throbbing of the engines just beneath my feet, I was soon down below at my reserved seat next to the head. I would have preferred to get sick over the side, but when you're five and the boat is rolling a lot, there is always the possibility of falling overboard. And after you have vomited once or twice into the wind, a toilet bowl, although full of unpleasant associations, seems almost like an old friend.

I didn't see anything that happened topside that day. I slept through it all, except when they brought me lunch, an act of intended kindness which seemed cruel at the time. The first couple of times I got sick, back in Key West, papa had returned and put me ashore. But I sensed there was something undignified about that, and also that the adults didn't like missing half a day's fishing. I was determined to lick the problem and I guess that even then I was trying to imitate my father's stoicism.

I woke up when we came into the harbor at the end of the day. When I staggered up onto the deck, I found everyone elated about something.

Then I saw what all the fuss was about. Half of Bimini was out on the dock, crowded around the biggest fish I had ever seen. They had him hung up, tail first, from a crossbeam and he must have been ten feet long. He looked three times the size of the natives gathered around him.

Everyone was congratulating papa. Mike not only thought that it was an extraordinary feat but that it would do a lot for Bimini, now that fishermen knew that tuna could be brought up unmutilated. Good old Mike, always unselfish and willing to share his private paradise with strangers for the sake of the islanders and their economy.

Their economy! That was sort of a bad joke. It consisted of three half-empty hotels kept going by their bar profits, a few sponge fishermen working the Great Bahama Bank, and a native straw market. There were a lot of pleasant blacks sitting around playing dominoes, always willing to help bait your fish hook and always full of great plans, though they never seemed to do anything.

To liven up this sad economy, and for reasons known only to his unconscious, papa started the weekly Saturday night fights. He offered the sum of one hundred dollars to any native who could last three rounds in the ring with him.

As papa later told me, once the word got around the Bahamas by motor and sail, the only means of communication in those days, giant blacks would come from as far away as Nassau, wait on the dock until he had returned from a day's fishing, and say, "I would like to try you this Saturday, Mr. Ernest."

Perhaps true, perhaps only partly true. My father had a tendency to improve on even the best of real stories. There's a picture in Carlos Baker's biography of papa that shows him boxing with a black who looks fair-sized. But when I met the same man in 1964, shortly before his death, I found that he wasn't any bigger than I, about five-feet-nine. Now we know that men shrink slightly with age, as their lower vertebrae dry out and are compressed by the weight of the rest of the body — but Jesus, not that much, not enough to make that guy, who was renowned in Bimini for his toughness in the ring, a worthy opponent of a man six feet tall and two hundred pounds.

I can remember the fights — the big crowd gathered around the ring on Saturday night, and the local announcer introducing the fighters:

"In dis corna, wearing white trunks, weighing almost two hundred and fifty pound, the scourge of the Bahamas, frightening Fighting Bob."

Loud cheers for the black plus a few shouts of restrained encouragement: "Knock the gentleman's block off, Bob."

"And in dis corna, wearing black trunks, at two hundred pounds, unequaled and undefeated in his last ten matches for the Heavyweight Cham-pee-anship of Bimini, that millionaire playboy and sportsman, Mr. Ernest Hemenway." The crowd goes wild.

"Kill him, Mr. Ernest, kill him. Send that nigger back to Nassau on ice. Kill him."

The fighters come out to the center of the ring and touch gloves. Papa lands a jab, a hard left, then an overhand right — Fighting Bob's stunned, he's covering up. Now a combination of rights and lefts, the crowd's on its feet, screaming — God, papa's throwing punches so fast I can't keep up with them. Then a *hard* looping right to the jaw and —

"Bob's down — Ladies and Gentlemen, Fighting Bob's down, and it doesn't look like he'll get up in time." The referee's signaling with his arms. It's all over.

Okay, the scene sounds real enough. But can I really remember that much or am I just imagining it? As I recall, the ring was elevated above the ground, floodlit, which would have cost a lot of money. And it was outdoors, and that beautiful ring, unless it was religiously looked after, wouldn't have lasted long with the heavy rains they have in Bimini. And nothing in Bimini was really looked after for long.

As I try to remember, try to get it just right, the mental image that comes to mind looks suspiciously like George Bellows' painting of Firpo knocking Dempsey through the ropes. So don't count on a five-year-old's memory to clarify a legend.

But the fights, with the then princely purse of one hundred dollars, did take place. I've verified that by questioning numerous people who were not aged five at the time and who did see them. And you know, it is something to issue a challenge to an island, and ultimately to the whole Bahamas, that you could knock out anybody before the end of three rounds. Sure, it was Hemingway, the twentieth-century Byron, overcompensating for being dressed as a girl for the first two years of his life. Maybe he was protesting his virility too much. I can't forget the reaction of Marjorie Kinnan Rawlings, the author of *The Yearling*, who visited my father in Bimini. They got along wonderfully, but when she left she said to my brother Jack:

"Why does a man with such great talent continually deny his sensitivity and overprotest his masculinity? He is so virile and so vast — why does he waste his time roughhousing with playboys, trying to catch the biggest fish, to bring that fish in the fastest, to drink the most? I know he loves to write, and why doesn't he spend more time at that?" Right on, Ms. Rawlings, you're probably 90 percent correct! But my father wrote a steady four to five hours almost every day of his life. He couldn't write fiction eighteen hours a day, it would have been just too exhausting.

Those Bimini bouts have often made me wonder how good a

fighter my father really was. He talked a lot about "cooling" people in bars with one punch, and slugging it out toe to toe with Tom Heeney on the beach at Bimini, right after Heeney had fought Gene Tunney, and Tom saying, "Let's stop this, Ernest, we're not getting paid."

Of course, I took it all as gospel truth because my father never lied to me. But you can knock a lot of people out with one punch if they give you the chance to land it just right — and you can box with a professional and finish feeling elated if the professional decides to carry you. All the professionals I've ever boxed with took it easy on me, mainly because I offered them no real competition, but also because the law considers their fists lethal weapons.

How good was my father, really? Well, I never saw him hit anyone, if you discount those half memories of Bimini, but I did see him box more than fifty rounds at various times with a gentleman named George Brown. No one ever hit George Brown except when he allowed it. My father could hit hard, if you stood still and gave him a target, so George never allowed it. I saw papa hit George's gloves many times but never saw him hit George.

Few people outside of boxing have ever heard of George Brown, but his name is legendary in the trade. He trained Harry Greb, perhaps the greatest middleweight of all time. He also trained Gene Tunney for a while, and as Mr. Tunney is still alive at this writing, he can vouch for George's skills.

Today George, who was originally a light heavyweight, weighs about 180 pounds, five pounds over his normal fighting weight. He has never smoked and he only holds cocktails at parties out of deference to his host. He is getting on now though he still jogs around Central Park reservoir in New York with me. But he never turns on the speed since he knows I smoke and he's much too considerate to hurt my feelings by beating a man half his age. He could have been light heavy-weight champion of the world but he knew that people took most of a fighter's money in those days, cut him up like a piece of pie, and he was too smart for that. Instead, he opened George Brown's Gymnasium, on 57th Street, where he helped women lose weight, and built up millionaires' egos by letting them hit him in the gut — and by calling them Sir, but never, if you listened closely, with much conviction.

He knew and boxed with and perhaps even loved my father over a twenty-five-year span. He drove the car back from the Mayo Clinic the last time and was asleep in the guest house when the shot went off that Sunday morning. I talked with George recently and here is an expert's opinion on my father as a fighter and as a boxer — there is a difference.

"Your father probably could have beaten up all those giant blacks in Bimini, Gregory — unless they knew something about boxing, which was unlikely, or unless papa came up against someone with great natural talent, like Greb. In Bimini your father would have been the one-eyed man in the kingdom of the blind.

"Unlike your father, I never had to teach Harry Greb any-thing. Just tried to keep him in shape. And away from women. If you didn't watch him, Harry would have a girl in his dressing room before a fight! Greb swarmed all over his opponent, like Joe Frazier used to do, but Harry was also the greatest dirty fighter who ever lived. Elbows, thumbs, knees, head — Greb used everything.

"Your father knew all those dirty tricks, too, and he continually used them on me. But he was too slow to implement them properly. You see, no one can learn to box, or even to use dirty tricks unless they have the tools. By that, I mean a person can't put into practice what they've been taught unless they have good coordination and reflexes, and your father didn't have either.

"But he must have been a good barroom fighter, especially if he could get in that first punch, because he was strong as an ox. But he was too slow for the ring, and I can think of hundreds of 'gentlemen' boxers, rich men who never had the need to fight professionally, and thousands of pros, who could have destroyed him.

"I think he probably did fight Tom Heeney on the Bimini beach, but I'm sure Tom carried him. I knew Tom for years when he had a bar in Miami, and he was a nice guy.

"Frankly, what amazed me about your father and made me sort of admire him, was that he persisted in trying his dirty tricks on me, even after I'd punished him severely for doing it. I had to dump him on his ass at least four times. He'd knee me and once he brought that pile-driving fist down on top of my head during a clinch. Christ, he tried everything he knew on me!

"Another time, after we'd finished boxing at my gym, papa went into the steam room and read the paper. I started into the room after he'd been in there for a while, and from the door I saw him folding up his paper, the short way, and pounding it into his fist.

"I thought, well he knows that one too. Then he came over to me and put one hand on my shoulder and said, 'How's it going, George?' at the same time jabbing the newspaper hard into my side. I was furious and I hit him so hard with my fist that when he fell, his head hit the tile of the steam room floor. Then I called in one of the weight lifters who worked at the gym to put him under the shower. I was so mad I wouldn't touch him.

"He wrote me a couple of months later about getting tickets to a fight he wanted to see and never mentioned the incident. Several months later we just took up where we left off, with him fumblingly trying to get at me and me just keeping him away, spinning him off balance, tying him up in clinches, giving him a workout — just tiring him without hurting him, like I did with all the other gentlemen.

"Of course, we both knew he liked to win. Yet he didn't feel he had to win at *everything*. He could readily accept that you were a better shot, Gig, or that Patrick was a better painter. But he had to win at boxing. The compulsion was so strong that it destroyed his judgment, and made him think he could beat a pro. Ridiculous! Can you imagine me challenging him to a winner-take-all contest in short story writing. You might get the impression that I didn't like your father in the ring and you'd be right. He was like a spoiled child when he boxed, whose manners had to be corrected constantly.

"But outside the ring, for most of his life, he was one of the finest men I've ever known."

Of course, other things happened in Bimini besides my father's making the residents punch drunk. I'd go play on the beautiful sandy beach with Ada, I'd watch the millionaires' yachts as they anchored offshore, particularly Bill Leeds' *Moana*, which was about 200 feet long and much too big for the Bimini harbor.

I'd hear stories, too, about Cat Cay, the millionaires' island, two miles farther south on the Bahama Bank. They said only millionaires and their friends were allowed there, and I never got to see it then.

But I visited Cat Cay about seven years ago and all the beautiful homes were still there, looking very South-of-France. Though they were boarded up, they were almost all in excellent repair, with only a few shutters banging occasionally to break the silence. The two caretakers kept the eight-hole golf course well-watered and mowed, and at any moment you expected a young couple, the man dressed in white ducks and blue blazer and the lovely young lady in an ankle-length skirt and early Duchess of Windsor coiffure, to come gaily hand in hand out of one of these houses, carefree, charming, and casual as only the really rich can be.

But the original rich have left Cat Cay or are dead, and their descendants have found or been led to places that are more fashionable now, leaving these great depreciating tax shelters behind. You can buy the island complete with houses for about two million now, if you have the money and want to be alone.

Whenever I think of Bimini, Mike Lerner is the man I remember best after papa. I never thought of Mike as a millionaire, just as a fine fisherman, though of course he was both. Years later, in 1964, I met him again in Bimini, sitting in a room with the blinds still drawn at midday.

Although I'd been back to the island several times, I'd never run into Mike. But his love and concern for the place were evident almost everywhere you looked. There was the Lerner house, no longer lived in and evidencing benign tropical neglect, but still the most beautiful home on the island. And there were the Lerner Marine Research Laboratories, where virologists from the University of Miami, including Dr. Benjamin Seigel, are doing original research on fish cancers and their relation to the disease in humans. (Did you know that fish can get cancer? I didn't until Dr. Seigel told me.)

But let's get back to Mike Lerner in that dark room, looking like death, and remembering happier times.

"There are so many things I'd like to tell you about your father, Gregory," he said. "God, we had fun in those days! We rode out a hurricane together in 'thirty-five or 'thirty-six and Ernest told such fascinating stories while the wind was tearing at the house that I forgot my fear. Although I'm sure that with that imagination of his, he was just as frightened. He must have remembered what a big blow did to Matecumbe Key in 'thirty-four, when all those bonus marchers were drowned in their encampment. But there isn't much time left, and I know you've got to get the plane back to Miami. Let me tell you just this one.

"Your father was broke in 'thirty-four or 'thirty-five, he'd spent a lot of time working on *Death in the Afternoon* and it hadn't sold. Of course, your mother had plenty of money but Ernest didn't like to use that unless he had to. I knew he was broke and I tried to think of some way to help him out.

"One morning I told him, 'Ernest, I've found a great stock, the Wall Street boys have missed it somehow, and the president of the company just wrote me to say they're going to announce in the next two weeks the discovery of oil on some land his firm owns. Teapot Dome, Inc., or whatever its name is, is sure to go as high as a gusher blowing wild when that announcement is made. If you've got some extra cash you don't know what to do with, I'll buy a hundred shares for you.

"Ernie was delighted and got five hundred dollars from your mother. Within three weeks I was able to give him back a check for five thousand dollars as the stock had gone up tenfold after the company president made his announcement."

Mike was smiling now, and remembering it all, his eyes had come to life, and he said:

"Of course, there wasn't any stock, Gregory, ever, except that damn oil stock of mine that never moved, which I sold to get the five thousand for your father."

Papa was anti-Semitic, but he had a knack for choosing friends who proved exceptions to his rule.

Sun Valley

WE REALLY HAD carte blanche in Sun Valley in the summer and fall of 1940, the first summer we spent with papa after Mother divorced him. Under the arrangement he had worked out with its owners, the Union Pacific, papa and his family would live in Sun Valley and the railroad could tell the literate world that he was there, and could take a reasonable number of pictures of the Hemingways at play. In return for this everything was on the house.

"Just sign for what you want, Gig. They have to keep a record of it for something they call Books — " papa laughed — "but it doesn't matter how much you spend. Just sign for it."

I remember resenting signing. Hell, if it was all free why did I have to sign? I was slow to learn to read, and even writing my name was still difficult at age nine. But then I began to discover what fun signing could be, and my penmanship improved.

Papa was jamming hard to finish *For Whom the Bell Tolls,* and with my brothers doing the more exciting things that older boys always do, I was left pretty much on my own. On a typical day I would wake up a little hung over from drinking what was left in the adults' glasses. I was staying in the Challenger Inn, which was much less posh than papa and Marty's suite in the Lodge. But there was no law that said I had to eat at the Inn's coffee shop, so I would have breakfast at the Ram Restaurant, which was more expensive and generally frequented by the Lodge's guests. I might order a fresh trout or Eggs Benedict. Then I would take some rolls from the table, and go outside for about an hour to feed the tame mallard ducks that lived on the pond beside the restaurant.

At first the ducks looked pretty much alike, the males with green heads and the females brown all over. But after a while I learned to distinguish them and even had names for some, like Quacker or Brownie. Eventually they got to know me, too, and would come when I called. There were few other children at Sun Valley that summer, most of them came and went so fast that you didn't get to know them, and so the ducks became my real playmates.

After an hour with the ducks, the bowling alley would open and I'd go roll a few games. Then I'd have a swim in the circular outdoor heated pool. It had glass walls, and with the steam rising up off the top of the water and swirling about in great clouds, it looked like something one dreams about, the under-world or the River Styx.

After the swim I'd have a massage, then go for a skeet-shooting lesson with a man they called The Little Colonel, a fat little fellow with a goatee. He would stand behind you and tell you how much to lead and when to pull the trigger. He was an incredible shot, but not much of a teacher because you couldn't hit a thing without him behind you.

My morning might end on the outdoor skating rink, where the local version of Sonja Henie would hold me close while she guided me through the figures. Having worked up a good appetite, I would go back to the Ram and have a steak or frogs' legs or guinea hen under glass, the last brought in with considerable ceremony, though I didn't find it as exciting as the flaming shish kebob.

After lunch I would feed the ducks again. Then I might go fishing in the artificial lake which was always stocked with young, inexperienced trout that would take any lure. Finally, perhaps a trip over to the stables for a ride before dinner with papa and Marty.

I had to be careful when Marty was around because she was acting in my mother's place and felt it her duty to enforce discipline. I soon sensed that when I whipped out my pencil, she didn't always approve of what I ordered, so whenever I ate with her I'd order something simple.

But I'd gladly miss the better dishes for a chance to be with Marty. She was a beautiful girl in 1940 and, amazingly, is even more beautiful now. Her hair was honey blond then, cut shoulder length, and she had a way of tossing it when she talked, not unlike a filly in a pasture tossing her mane. I can't remember the color of Marty's eyes, but they were warm and mischievous simultaneously and sparkled when she smiled. And her skin was like Ingrid Bergman's — fresh and clear, with a glow of perpetual health and purity.

She could talk of anything — or nothing if you wished. She'd been to Spain and China and just about every other place, it seemed, and she'd talk to you like an equal, listen to your nine-year-old's opinions, and at least pretend to give them weight.

(When I met her in Boston about seven years ago, she was still a gorgeous woman, though she must have been in her late fifties by then. I confess that I thought momentarily about trying to posthumously cuckold papa. He couldn't be hurt anymore and, besides, we'd always shared everything. But Marty would have just laughed that wonderfully abandoned, sinful, yet perfectly pure laugh — I miss you too, Marty.)

But I must get back to that summer and fall of 1940. The bill for all my signing in the first month came to about $600. Papa called me into his room. I was scared. Although he was always gentle with me, his size alone was intimidating.

"Gig, I haven't taught you anything about the value of money. Basically, it's worthless, but it lets you buy a lot of things that you can enjoy. When you sign for things here, it's just like spending the nickels and dimes I give you for pocket money. We won't always have this much, so enjoy it while you can.

"I'm not saying this will spoil you for good or permanently ruin your sense of values. You'll find out soon enough how difficult money is to come by and you'll shepherd what you have when you're older and can add."

Then papa came to the point. "That nice man, Mr. Anderson, the one who runs this place, is a little pissed off," papa said. "He says you've set some sort of record for a nine-year-old in one month. Even the Aga Khan's kid only spent two hundred dollars the month he was here." Papa laughed, then added, in a more serious voice, "We might have to leave if you keep this up."

My face fell — who would feed the ducks?

"Mr. Anderson didn't say we'd *have* to leave, but he asked

me to talk to you. So try to keep the signing down. Don't order such fancy things and take it easy on the skeet and skating lessons. The pheasant and duck shooting will start soon and I'll take you out with us when we go. That, at least, will make up for the skeet shooting you'll miss. Live birds are more fun, anyway.

"You can eat pretty much what you want but no more guinea hen under glass or that flaming meat on a stick. The swimming and bowling are okay, though, and you can fish and ride as much as you want. Just take it a little easier, pal. You certainly wouldn't want to embarrass the family and get us thrown out on our ass, would you?"

So I cut down. The next month I lowered my bill to under $300, and although still less than delighted, papa could always recognize improvement. It meant I could not only keep my friends the ducks but protect my family from permanent disgrace.

The duck shooting started in the fall and as papa had talked my mother into letting me miss a few weeks of school, I was able to stay for some of it.

It was strange at first. The dead ducks looked so much like my friends, except that the dead ones usually had blood all over their feathers and didn't move or quack. But I suppressed the association.

Papa didn't deliver any pious lectures about giving them the "gift of death" or any of that crap he talked in later years when he was sick and tired and death may have appeared to be a gift. The only thing I remember was his advice when we picked up a wounded duck: "Wring its neck quickly so it won't suffer."

I became inured to killing at an early age and for a while later on out in Africa, I was like that character in "The Short Happy Life of Francis Macomber" who would kill anything, absolutely anything. But not anymore. I can even feel the life in a great tree now, and I wince when I see one girdled and know it must die. Perhaps the gift of death is getting too close to me.

All kinds of people would go shooting with us that fall. Gary Cooper was the one I liked best. I'd seen a lot of his movies and he was no different in person than he was in them — unbelievably handsome, gentle, courteous, and innately noble.

I remember one day after shooting we were in a general store and an old lady recognized Coop and asked him for his autograph.

"I just love your movies, Mr. Cooper. And you know why? You're always the same in them."

Coop just smiled, signed, and said, "Thank you, ma'am."

Being told your performances never change from picture to picture isn't exactly a compliment for an actor. Papa swore Coop never caught this nuance, but I wonder. He told that story about the old lady time and again, but never to Coop and never with any malice. There was little malice in my father in those days.

Papa and Coop talked a lot during lunch on our pheasant shoots, for the most part casual conversation about hunting and Hollywood. Though they had little in common intellectually, a kindness and gentleness seemed to exist between them. And they really did enjoy each other — you could tell by the resonance of their voices and the way their eyes smiled. And there was nobody around to impress, that was the beauty of it, just their wives and kids. Maybe that seems an unkind thing to say, but both of them were great actors (yes, my father was one) who had forged, consciously or otherwise, two of the most

Papa displays some trophy heads in Africa. The year was 1933, he was on the safari that he described in *Green Hills of Africa,* and he had just lost forty pounds after a bout of dysentery. *Collection of Mary Hemingway*

I was nine years old when Papa took us to Sun Valley for the summer.
I used to feed tame ducks every afternoon — but killing wild ones didn't
seem to bother me. *Lloyd Arnold*

A year later this photo of Papa and me was taken during a Sun Valley
hunting trip.   *Lloyd Arnold*

In 1946, my half-brother Jack (left) was photographed on the Sun Valley
ski slopes with Ingrid Bergman, Gary Cooper, and Clark Gable.

Lloyd Arnold

Papa measures the antler spread of my brother Pat's first big game kill—an Idaho mule deer buck, which he shot in October 1966.   *Lloyd Arnold*

A recent photograph of my wife Valerie and myself, and three of my seven children. From left: Sean, Vanessa, and Edward.   *Frank Worth*

successful hero images of this century. There was never rivalry between them, and there was no reason for any. They were both at their peak then.

Though I was just a kid, I never thought Coop was as dumb as a lot of people claimed. Nor did I think that he was "real folks" or merely an uncommonly handsome common man, a Mr. Deeds who had gone to Hollywood. Remember that he was the son of a Montana State Supreme Court judge, and had been educated in the East. To put my feelings in the vernacular that he used (I won't say "affected"), he was just real nice to be around.

Coop was an excellent rifle shot, as good or maybe even better than my father. But the very steadiness, the deliberate strength that made him one made him a slow shotgun shot. Papa was the same way — an excellent rifle, fair shotgun, shot. But I think papa's problem was his vision because he took such a long time to pick up a bird in his sights. As a result he sometimes made tough shots out of easy ones, just as an outfielder who is slow getting the jump on a ball will make a spectacular diving catch, when all he needed to do was start a little sooner.

Ingrid Bergman was out there, too. I had been raised a Catholic — Mother's religion — and I first glimpsed Miss Bergman at Mass one Sunday that fall. She was sitting at the front of the church, and I couldn't see her face. But I noted how her arm reached, with the grace of a ballerina's, across two worshippers to drop an offering in the basket. I waited until Mass was out to get a full view of her. Her face shone, it actually radiated. I'd seen her in *Intermezzo,* at a private screening for papa, but she was five times more beautiful in the flesh than she was in the film.

Some women are noted for producing a state of temporary insanity in their admirers, but with Miss Bergman the insanity was permanent. Alas, it was almost impossible to get close to her, as she was always surrounded by men like Howard Hawks, Gary Cooper, or my father. It was fun to watch them make fools of themselves in her presence. I'm not at all implying she wasn't smart — I never really got a chance to talk to her — but she'd say something inane like "I always carry an extra pair of stockings in my bag because you're always getting runs in them and where can you find a pair in the middle of an evening?"

And papa, whose only possible interest in her lingerie was how to get it off her, would say, "Yes, Ingrid, that's a very practical thing to do, very practical. It shows you have real common sense, daughter."

And then everyone would go back to staring at her until she spoke again.

Her husband, Peter Lindstrom, must have had a hard time. He was extremely nice, but nobody seemed to notice him. They called him Mr. Bergman behind his back. He was actually a fine neurosurgeon, and possibly more talented and worthwhile in his own right than all the others put together. He had a warm smile and he liked to talk to kids. Maybe he couldn't get near Miss Bergman either, and was lonely. I prefer to think he was just nice, like Coop.

When the fall was over, I had to go back to Key West, back to the heat, to Mother, to school. I don't think that summer spoiled me for life, but it made a lot of other things dull by comparison.

Havana

After my parents were divorced, and my father remarried, he moved to Cuba. Marty found them a wonderful old house about nine miles outside of Havana. It was situated on twenty acres of some of the loveliest land I've seen. Mango trees lined the driveway leading up to the house, and tall royal palms grew beside the path leading down to the swimming pool in back. Flowers and bougainvillea vines bloomed all over. Humming-birds made their tiny neat square nests in the tropical foliage, and I could watch for hours a mother sitting on her eggs, one of the most regally beautiful sights I've ever seen. The rambling, one-story Spanish colonial house was perched on the highest point of land in the area, and had a wonderful view of the lights of Havana. It was called Finca Vigía, or Lookout Farm, though we simply called it the Finca.

It was hard to believe that anyone could produce in such a place, and for many of the years that I visited Havana, I never thought of my father as a working writer. I knew that he had written books in the past, because he was Hemingway the

Writer; but I never saw him at work, and I had doubts mixed with hero worship. Although I suppressed them as much as possible, they kept popping to the surface. Was he a phony? He was always talking about his work but when did he do it?

I'd get up around eight-thirty during those summer vacations, have a leisurely breakfast, and then a swim. By the time I made it up to the big house around ten, there was papa, a Scotch and soda in his hand, bidding me a cheerful good morning.

"What do you want to do today, Gig? I haven't planned anything definite yet. Maybe we could have lunch at the Floridita, and then shoot a few practice pigeons in the afternoon. Gregorio called to say it's too rough for fishing. When he cancels this early it means the winds already are at gale force and the sea will be rough all day. Think about it, and then we'll make definite plans.

"Maybe we should just take it easy today," he would say, looking closer at me with concern. "You don't look so good. Are you coming down with something, old pal?"

"I feel like I'm coming up with something, papa. It almost feels like I'm seasick."

"I'll fix you a bloody mary. You've just got a hangover." He would sound relieved. From the time I was ten or eleven, he let me drink as much as I wanted, having confidence that I would set my own limits.

"Maybe you should cut down on the drinking? If you don't —" his voice rose in mock seriousness — "discipline must be enforced. We can't send you back to Mother at the end of the summer with the D.T.'s."

We'd usually have been up fairly late drinking the night before and I would think I'd done pretty well to be awake by eight-thirty. My head may have been buzzing, but I was still up. My father would always look great, as if he'd slept a baby's sleep in a soundproof room with his eyes covered by black patches. Sometimes I could explain it to myself satisfactorily, remembering how he'd fallen asleep with the Scotch in his hand going down slowly to rest on the arm of the chair. But more often there just wasn't any explanation, except, as I learned, his remarkable metabolism. I was certain he hadn't gotten up before me. But he had.

It was his habit, my older brothers later told me, to get up every morning of his adult life around five-thirty or six, when the first light woke him. He'd work for four or five hours. If, after a couple of hours, he saw that his writing wasn't going well he'd knock off the serious stuff and answer letters. He loved writing letters, because they gave him a chance to relax from "the awful responsibility of writing," or, as he sometimes called it, "the responsibility of awful writing." In his letters he didn't have to worry about how a passage sounded or was constructed, and he could joke and gossip and give well-intended (and usually solicited) advice.

In the summers when Pat and I were there — Jack had gone into the army — papa would, apparently, quit earlier in the morning, to have more time with us. But I knew none of this then and to me he was just a rich playboy who spent most of the day with us children, swimming, playing tennis or baseball, shooting, fishing, and going to Havana.

Most evenings we would go to the Fronton for the jai alai, which is one of the most aesthetically rewarding games you can ever hope to see. The players are superb natural athletes and the grace and agility they display, literally climbing the walls to make a shot, makes you gasp just as you do when Nureyev makes a *grand jeté* and seems to hang in the air for an instant. But unlike ballet, jai alai has a considerable element of danger: the ball sometimes travels at well over a hundred miles an hour, is harder than a baseball, and can kill a player if it hits him.

In jai alai, a player throws the ball against the front wall of a three-sided rectangular concrete court with a curved hollowed-out basketlike apparatus attached to his hand; it is roughly five feet long and shaped like a scythe or a macaw's bill. Then the opposing player has to try to catch the ball in the tip of that bill, let it roll down to the center of the basket and, all in the same motion, propel it back to the wall. If the player drops the ball he not only loses the point but causes the odds to change.

Betting was great fun because you placed your wager in a tennis ball with a hole in it and threw it down to the bookmaker, who threw your receipt back; then you returned the ball to him. I loved to throw the balls back and forth even if I didn't always understand the intricacies of the betting. The odds changed throughout the thirty-point match and they varied with each point and with the fortunes of the two teams. You could start betting on team A (call them the Colts) and if it fell behind, you could put a large bet on team B (say, the Giants), not at very good odds, but what you won would be enough to cover your bet on the Colts if they lost. Then, if the Colts drew even and looked as though they might win, you could bet on them again and you could end up winning if the Colts won and not losing if they lost.

Papa knew all the jai alai players personally, and had had most of them out to the Finca for drinks and a swim; knowing the players made the game much more fun to watch. We rarely lost money. Papa had one streak in which he won on twenty-nine straight games. This got around among the betting fraternity and people who had never heard of Ernest Hemingway the writer, types who looked as if they couldn't even read, would come up to him and tug at his coat, to ask his advice. He would readily provide it, but since it was impossible to follow all his bets as the match progressed, he wasn't really a good tout.

Papa also took me to my first cockfight, a Havana spectacle which the greed of the gamblers damned for me. It just didn't seem to belong to the realm of sport.

I remember watching once while a badly wounded fighting chicken was placed on a white line at the center of the ring. As long as it could manage to stay put, its backers wouldn't lose. One eye was shut, the other closing, and a chest wound was slowly draining it of life. The bird wobbled and fell. Its handler picked it up and gave it emergency first aid — and then put it back in the fight. It took more punishment, wobbled, and fell again.

This time the handler pleaded with cock's backer not to force him to put the dying bird back on the line. "Enough is enough!" he shouted. "Let's kill it or take it out of the ring. A vet may stop the bleeding before it's too late."

But the backer refused. I don't think that he was inordinately bloodthirsty. It was just that he hoped that if he prayed to his favorite saint, did a penance, or promised not to cheat on his wife, his luck would change, his bird would recover — and he wouldn't lose his money!

At least, that's the way papa explained it to me.

Unusual things always seemed to happen in Havana. Once, when we were driving at a snail's pace through the crowded, narrow back streets of the city, shots rang out and a man came running toward us with a submachine gun. He said to our chauffeur, Juan, as he handed him the gun, "Hold this for me, will you please? I have to run."

Juan was too surprised to do anything else; but papa, who was sitting next to him in the open Lincoln convertible, cursed at him under his breath. "You've got your prints all over it now, you bloody fool. Wipe it off and drop it, and let's get the hell out of here."

An apocryphal tale, you say? I swear it happened. I never learned who the unlucky target was, and the gun wasn't ever connected with Juan. I guess it must have been a political shooting, because the news about it was suppressed.

When we went to the Floridita bar in those days it wasn't like Orson Welles entering the lobby of the Grand Hotel, as Hotchner described papa's public excursions in later years. It was just a nice bar where my father knew the staff and could drink with us and his friends. Occasionally somebody would recognize him and rush out to buy a copy of one of his books and ask him to autograph it. Papa would usually inquire whether there was anything special they wanted written, and if there wasn't he would make up something funny and sign it.

There were no fights and few scenes at the Floridita, and what scenes there were usually ended with papa whispering something in the troublemaker's ear, at which the man would turn white and leave.

"I whisper in their ear, Gig, to stop fights before they start. That way you avoid unpleasantness and lawsuits." But he never said what he whispered in their ear.

When we didn't eat at the Floridita, we'd sometimes make reservations for a feast at a Chinese restaurant called El Pacifico. It was on the top floor of a five-story building and to get to it you had to go up in an old elevator with a sliding iron grille for a door. It stopped at every floor whether you wanted it to or not. On the second floor there was a five-piece Chinese orchestra blaring crazy atonal music. This either got you in a Far Eastern mood or gave you a headache, depending on how long the elevator stopped. Then you reached the third floor, where there was a whorehouse, and the girls would smile and wave. The fourth floor was an opium den with pitifully wasted little figures curled up around their pipes, oblivious to everything.

You'd have forgotten all about eating by the time you reached the top floor where the sprawling Chinese restaurant was located under an awning, with a fine view of Havana. Men hunching over bowls of rice and talking incredibly fast with mouths full would look up momentarily at our party and then go to shoveling down food. I've never seen people eat so fast or so volubly. We always had a big table with many lavish courses and I remember feeling sorry for the Chinese eating just rice.

Shark fin soup was always the first course. As I'd seen a lot of sharks, and mostly just their fins, I couldn't imagine eating one. But the fin wasn't bad at all, and had a peculiar texture that crushed soothingly in your mouth.

Papa would tell how he had eaten monkey brains right out of the monkey's skull when he was in China. He also described how one day as he was walking down the street in Shanghai, he'd seen a policeman tie a man's hands behind his back, order him to get on his knees, and then, taking a pistol out of his holster, shoot the man in the ear. No crowd had collected and the man didn't resist. Through his interpreter, papa asked the policeman what the man had done. The policeman answered that he had caught him selling dope, that this was an offense punishable by death, and that the courts were too crowded for such common cases.

"Quick justice is best," the policeman told papa. It may have been fascinating conversational fare, but I didn't order brains that day.

When we had finished one of these huge feasts, we'd go slowly down past the dope fiends, past the girls still smiling and waving, past the cacophonous noises of the Chinese orchestra. El Pacifico was a strange, romantic place to visit, but it was a relief to get out into the light of the street and to be in the West again.

The first summer that really stands out was the summer of '42. That was the summer when papa taught me to shoot. He belonged to a posh shooting club, the Club de Cazadores del Cerro, about five miles from the Finca. The club had facilities for every kind of shooting: trap, skeet, rifle, and live pigeons.

The live pigeon shooting is the most exciting. A pigeon is catapulted from an open underground trench about twenty yards away. It can come from any of five equidistant catapults in the trench, and you have to bring it down before it flies over a circular fence which, at its farthest, is about forty yards from you. Papa said he had done this kind of shooting in San Sebastian in Spain where the top prizes and side bets often were in the tens of thousands of dollars. *That* was real dough, and I kept thinking that here was my chance to break into the big money.

But I couldn't hit anything at first.

"Don't worry about hitting the pigeons, Gig, just concentrate on your form," papa would tell me. "If you fire enough shots you'll start to get the leads down, that is, you'll learn how far to fire in front of a bird flying at an angle to you. The shot doesn't get there as soon as the gun goes off, you know. It seems like it does, but it takes a half second or so to reach the bird, depending on how fast he's flying, how far away he is, the strength of the powder charge, and a few other factors.

"But I'm only confusing you with all this explanation. Just concentrate on your form now. You're right-handed, so put the stock of the gun firmly against your right shoulder, make sure it feels comfortable, and that all the stock is up against your shoulder. If the gun isn't positioned correctly, a smaller percentage of your shoulder will receive its full recoil, and it will kick like hell. Then you'll start to flinch, jerking the trigger in anticipation of the pain of the recoil, and that will move your gun off target before the shot leaves the barrel.

"That's right, firm against the shoulder, keep your head down, weight on your left front foot, and close that left eye. I think you're ready for a twenty-gauge shotgun this year — at eleven you're big enough for one. It will kick a little at first but if you hold it properly you won't even notice it after a while. Honest." He smiled.

His instructions made sense, but it was a lot to remember all at once. The first time I fired the twenty-gauge I forgot to keep my weight forward and was so off balance leaning on my rear foot that the gun's recoil knocked me right on my behind. Everyone, especially my brother Pat, roared with laughter.

"That's okay, Gig," papa said. "It's the only way to learn,

and the next time I'm sure you'll keep your weight on your front foot. I think that's enough for today — I'm not a believer in the traumatic school of learning. Not because you couldn't take it, old pal, but a bad enough sore shoulder might make you develop a permanent flinch, and ruin you for good as a shooter. Just watch the way Pat and I do it for the rest of the day and keep going over and over in your mind the points I stressed."

Although I was driven to fanatical practicing, my shoulder hurt badly the first week. I couldn't hit anything. But once the pain went away, I started to hit a few birds.

Not many at first because you have to fire hundreds of shots before you unconciously learn to lead them. Anybody can tell you that if a bird is flying at 30 miles an hour at a certain angle twenty yards from you, you should lead him a foot, and keep swinging after you've fired, etc. But *exactly* how fast the bird is flying and at *exactly* what angle he is traveling relative to you can't be taught.

Papa seemed pleased with my progress the first month, and I placed second and third in a couple of minor shoots. He could see that I had the basic requirements for a good wing shot — quick reflexes and that x-factor that enables you to put together all the variables in your head in an instant.

"Don't get your hopes up too high, Gig, but I think you might have an outside chance in the Cuban championship this year. A lot of good shots will be there, but you've demonstrated on occasion that you can shoot with the best of them. It's a long ordeal. Each man has to shoot twenty birds, and there will be at least a half hour's wait between birds. The waiting is what's tough and if you haven't missed, the pressure of the waiting gets to you after the tenth bird. But everybody reacts to pressure in different ways, and you seem to thrive on it from what I've seen so far.

"And remember this, during the half hour wait between birds, most of the adults will be drinking to calm their nerves and the drinking will slow them up. You won't be taking anything but Coke." He smiled. "And don't drink much of that at any one time, either. Take a regular swig but don't swallow much, just wash it around in your mouth and spit it out."

"Where?" I asked.

"Don't worry, we'll get a bucket. The most important thing to remember, the thing which gives you an outside chance, is that there won't be much pressure on you because no one expects you to win. And no financial pressure, either — the cost of those expensive guns, the shells, and the birds, the big side bets these champions have between them. You've got none of those problems," he laughed. "And you might get hot; I've seen it happen before. You might get hot."

Despite what papa said, I was feeling a lot of pressure the day of the championship, and trying awfully hard not to show it. The contestants were auctioned off in a Monte Carlo pool, with 75 percent of the pool going to the winner and the rest to the second-place finisher. Some of the shooters, like Cappie Cruz, the former champion of both Cuba and Spain, went for as high as three or four hundred dollars.

Milling around with the crowd before the shoot began was the most fun. President Batista's Chief of Police was one of the shooters. He was pointed out to me, an innocuous-looking fellow, except that he wore the kind of dark glasses that reflected the light and didn't let you see his eyes.

Everybody was joking and reminiscing about past shoots.

But, of course, there was the usual percentage of grimly compulsive competitors, running polishing cloths again and again over their guns, watched by even more anxious wives and kids, who were periodically ordered to fetch something important from the car, to get them a drink, or to "just leave me alone!"

And of course there were the "peacock" shooters, as I called them, the gun-club enthusiasts who had so many patches on their shooting jackets, attesting to memberships in clubs and past triumphs, that they looked as though they were advertising cigars.

"Where'd you get that beautiful patch from, sir?" I asked one particularly intense looking gentleman.

"I got that one for killing thirty straight at Monte Carlo, son." Pigeons or people, I wondered.

I can't remember much of the beginning of the shoot, except that I had pretty easy birds at first and didn't miss any. But around the twelfth bird I had a real screamer. He caught the wind just right as he came out of the catapult and although my first shot missed, the second one got him; he bounced off the fence and fell on the inside.

When I returned to my seat next to papa I said, "I can't even remember shooting that second shot."

"Good. You're hot, you're doing it by instinct now. Have some Coke, old man, but spit it out in the bucket."

We must have looked pretty ridiculous sitting there — me swishing Coke around in my mouth and spitting it out and papa, with his chair turned toward me, keeping up a constant chatter about anything but shooting, trying to keep me from worrying.

By the seventeenth round only three of the original one hundred and fifty contestants were left, Mungo Perez, Cappie Cruz, and myself.

"Mungo's got a fat ass like a woman," I said, when he went out to shoot his eighteenth. "Have you ever noticed that? And Cappie's barely hit his last two. He's on his last legs. I can take them both."

"I can see you're going to be a gracious champion," papa said, smiling. "Try concentrating on hitting the next two and forget about your acceptance speech."

Then Cappie missed the nineteenth bird and the crowd seemed to let its breath out all at once. I heard a man behind me say, "Poor Mungo. If he loses, it's a disaster, and if he wins he's only beat a kid." Mungo hit his twentieth bird, however, and avoided the disaster.

Now it's my turn. The legs aren't there. I can't see too well. There must be sweat in your eyes, I think, rub it out. Get up, walk straight, for Christ's sake — they're applauding. Weight on the *front* foot, head down, cheek against the stock. Swing left, swing right, back to the center. Keep that head down. Aim just above the center trap. What the hell's coming out? Whoosh — an easy one. Swing in front of him, keep in front of him. Pull the trigger. Pull the goddamn trigger!

An instant later the whole place exploded — people rushed toward me, jumping the fence, and papa hugged me. At age eleven, I'd just tied for the shooting championship of Cuba against some of the best wing shots in the world. Minutes later at the bar I was explaining to a group of newly acquired admirers that it was really nothing if one had my 20/10 vision, fabulous reflexes, co-ordination, guts, and stamina. After listening to this as long as he could, papa took me aside and said:

"Gig, when you're truly great at something, and you know it, you would like to brag about it sometimes. But if you do, you'll feel like shit afterwards. Also, you never remember how a thing really felt if you talk about it too much." I took the hint and changed the subject fast.

The next day the sports sections of the Havana papers devoted whole pages to my achievement, going into minute details of my life without having asked me a single word about it. According to them, I was a straight A student, spoke flawless Spanish, showed my father's talent for creative writing, was kind to animals when I wasn't killing them, had excellent table manners, etc., etc. But my innate modesty, according to one particularly creative reporter, was such that it precluded discussing these virtues. However, this enterprising man said that he had questioned one of the "many" servants at my father's "country estate" and had been told that I never missed Mass on Sunday, that I always made my bed promptly in the morning and willingly helped with the household chores, never left any food on my plate and was polite, although never condescending, with all the servants, and was well liked by all my "less fortunate" playmates in the local village. In short, I was a Niño Modelo, a model child.

Papa had the three Havana dailies spread out on the floor in front of him and was roaring with laughter as he translated all this for me.

"Well, they're right about one thing, I've never seen anybody change the sheets faster than you after you've wet your bed. But Christ, these Cuban writers are something, Gig. Why would you bother to help with 'the household chores' if we had all those mythical servants that idiot is writing about? They're

trying to make you Cuba's first certified saint, El Virgen de la
Finca. Well, you do go to Mass every Sunday, they're right
there — unless, of course, you've got a terrible hangover," he
roared.

"Let me take a good look at you, modelo. Turn to the right,
that's your best profile." He was imitating a fag photographer
now, lisping, "thtop picking your nose, dear. How can I shoot
while you're picking your nose!"

Then more seriously:

"But we probably shouldn't be too hard on Cuban reporters — they just have a romantic view of life. And almost all
reporters are inaccurate. Have you ever noticed when you read
about something in the papers you truly know about that
ninety percent of it is inaccurate? A lot of mistakes have to do
with early deadlines, of course, the need to get something
down in a hurry for the afternoon or morning editions. Often
there's just no time to check the accuracy of your sources. I
know — I started out as a reporter on the Kansas City *Star*. But
some of it comes from the reporter's conceit, and the contempt
for a reader's intelligence that only a truly conceited reporter
can have. And a lot comes from laziness, or, to be more accu-
rate, from fatigue.

"This is a real education for you. I doubt I'll ever have to
worry about you believing your own clippings now, Gig.
Sorry: Niño Modelo. I forgot to address you by your proper
title."

It wasn't all fun and games in Havana that summer of '42.
There was a polio epidemic in the city, and I came down with a
sore throat and fever, and my legs ached and felt strange. Papa
put me in bed immediately and got two specialists from Havana

within an hour, one a neurologist and the other a renowned internist. And he put a cot in my room so he could be with me at night.

The doctors would come in from Havana twice a day, hitting my knees with a soft rubber hammer and watching my legs jump. Then they would go off in a corner and consult in whispers.

It went on like this for three days and it scared the hell out of me, the way they always smiled so kindly, were so solicitous, and kept tapping my knees with that hammer. I knew about the polio epidemic in Havana, and that I had the symptoms of the disease, a bad fever and aching leg muscles. Oh God, why wouldn't these nice, obviously competent men say something about my prognosis — something good like "You're going to get well, you won't be paralyzed for life." But I knew there must be some reason for their silence and that it wouldn't be smart to ask.

The table beside the bed was covered with medicines, all worthless of course, but evidence of their concern. Papa wouldn't allow anyone else in the room except himself and the doctors, and he took my temperature every four hours and brought my meals in himself.

He'd lie beside me on the cot at night telling wonderful stories about his life up in Michigan as a boy, how he'd caught his first trout and how beautiful the virgin forests were before the loggers came. He told me about the times he'd been scared as a boy, how he used to dream about a furry monster who would grow taller and taller every night and then, just as it was about to eat him, would jump over the fence. He said fear was perfectly natural and nothing to be ashamed of. The trick to mastering it was controlling your imagination; but he said he knew how hard that was for a boy.

He said he loved to read the Bible when he was seven or eight because it was so full of battles. "But I wasn't much good reading at first, Gig, just like you. It was years before I realized that 'Gladly, the cross I'd bear' didn't refer to a kindly animal. I could easily imagine a cross-eyed bear and Gladly seemed like such a lovely name for one."

Mainly he just told me stories — about how he had fished and hunted in the Michigan north woods and about how he wished he could have stayed my age and lived there forever — until I fell asleep.

And then the crisis passed and I got well and papa said, "Jesus Christ, we licked that one, Gig," and knocked on wood.

But, in fact, nobody licked polio before the Salk vaccine unless it was in the cards. Still, I feel that papa's tender loving care, confidence, and prayers didn't hurt.

There was one time, though, when he really may have saved my life that summer.

When we weren't fishing for marlin, we'd often use the *Pilar* for scuba diving, taking her out to little coral reefs offshore. We had none of the gear which is used in modern scuba diving. No air tanks or arbeletes or sophisticated fish-hunting weaponry — just goggles or, later, face masks and a spear that looked like Neptune's trident.

Mostly we speared yellowtail, snapper, and grunts. The latter are so named because they make an almost humanlike grunting sound when you take them out of the water. But just watching could be fun, too. Like whole fields of silvery mobiles, schools of fish would materialize and disappear as quickly as they had come. Barracudas, hanging absolutely still, would seem to defy all laws of gravity. Sometimes, the cudas would get quite close to you, as near as three or four feet away. They would stare at you and would open their mouths to show those great teeth; probably they were just yawning. The main danger from cudas, papa warned us, came when you entered the water near them too suddenly. Then they might make a slashing attack before running off, but not before they seemed to bow, Japanese-style, with half your thigh in their mouths.

There were stingrays as well, but they, too, were unconcerned with us. Nothing about the reef was really dangerous, except, perhaps, if you reached into a hole for a crawfish. These holes had to be probed with a spear first; sometimes moray eels hid in them and a big enough moray could take your hand off at the wrist if you bothered him in his territory.

All of the fish were supremely oblivious to scuba divers then. Even the majestic jewfish, which today is almost as sought after as the white whale, would just saunter by. I lost several spears on them because, although it was easy to hit these two- or three-hundred-pound monsters, they seemed merely to shrug and casually swim off with my spear in their side.

As I say, most of those days when we went spear fishing we'd anchor near a reef offshore. But sometimes we'd start off marlin fishing, and if our luck wasn't good in the morning, we'd have lunch on the *Pilar* and then go to a reef right on the edge of the Gulf Stream, as much as a mile or more from land. Because it was tiring for me to stay afloat for long periods, I preferred the shallow reefs inshore where I could touch bottom easily: I was only four and a half feet tall and there was usually a good five feet of water covering the outer reefs. Moreover, they were right on the edge of the Gulf Stream where the depth dropped off steeply on the ocean side to about 600 fathoms. I had heard a lot about the sea monsters that lived down there, and I decided to stay away from that edge.

One day the morning fishing had been lousy and we anchored off the deepwater reef in the afternoon. Papa's mate, Gregorio, would come partway out in the dinghy and take the fish off our spears. Because I was expending a lot of energy just staying afloat, I didn't return to the dinghy as often as papa, and I hit on an ingenious idea for storing the fish I had caught. I unbuckled my belt, passed one end in the mouth of the fish and out through his gills, and then rebuckled it. This way I could catch three or four fish before I had to make the forty- or fifty-yard swim back to the dinghy.

I'd had fair luck and had speared three or four grunts, when suddenly I noticed that there wasn't a fish in sight. I couldn't understand why, or where they had all gone. It hadn't seemed that there were enough holes in the coral to hold so many thousands of fish.

I was still pondering this problem when I looked out into the blue vastness of the Gulf Stream and saw why the fish had left. Three huge sharks, each more than eighteen feet long, were coming toward me in slow S-shaped curves, following the scent of the blood that had gone out into the deeper water.

I screamed as loudly as I could, uncontrollably, again and again, more terrified than I had ever been in my life. Even over the sound of the waves, my father could hear me.

"What is it, Gig?"

"Sharks, sharks — three big ones."

"Okay, pal, take it easy, throw something at them to get their attention, and swim to me."

I took the grunts off my belt and tossed them toward the sharks. Papa was about forty yards away, and although I wasn't much of a swimmer, I must have made it to him in near-record time. He lifted me up on his shoulders and then thrashed through the water to the dinghy. I looked back to see if the sharks were following us: across the reef I could see a disturbance in the water, with fins breaking the surface, where the sharks were eating the grunts.

I can't say with certainty that my father was very brave that day. He seemed cool enough, but I could tell he was frightened, too, as we made our way back to the dinghy. But he didn't break for the boat by himself when I yelled "shark." He also had the calmness to advise me to throw something in their direction.

I guess almost any man would have waited for a child, but I never felt more like his son than I did that day. Underneath the boisterous exterior, he was a reserved man, somewhat incapable of expressing his affection in the conventional way, and I hadn't realized how much he really cared until he hoisted me on his own shoulders, which were barely out of water, and swam back across that reef with most of his own body still exposed under the surface.

Papa really bawled me out when he discovered that I had kept the dead fish on my belt and it was their blood scent that had brought the sharks up from the depths of the Gulf Stream. We had been lucky. It was a hell of a story to tell your friends, and papa thrived on this kind of dangerous situation — as long as you managed to survive it. He frequently made use of real incidents like this in his work. I think this particular one formed the basis for a scene about a shark attacking my brother in *Islands in the Stream*. Papa almost always changed the situation a little and usually improved on it slightly but mainly he used material that had actually happened.

Sometimes, his sense of reality deserted him, or rather, reality and invention blended before he put the finished product down on paper. This could be dangerous, as you'll see in the next chapter.

Don Quixote vs.
The Wolf Pack

HAVE YOU EVER wondered whether your fishing boat, *your* boat, properly equipped and armed, and manned by a daredevil crew, could have sunk a Nazi submarine? You'll notice I use a past form of the subjunctive, the mood of doubt, in the last sentence. You see? *Could have.*

But let's go back in time, to 1943; wolf packs were running silently under the seas, menacing anything that passed over or near them. All right. Would you ever dare to take on a submarine with a fishing boat? No, that's absurd, you say, my boat's only fourteen feet long, with a 100-horsepower Merc. engine, and I couldn't possibly fit enough guns and crew — But wait. Say, for the sake of argument, that you have a larger boat. You've seen those, and maybe with a touch of envy, admired them. The forty-foot Bertrams. What lines, what speed, what class, what power! God, you'd give anything for one of those!

Then imagine that your wife talked you into buying a ticket in one of those crazy lotteries where the winner gets a million bucks. The odds are four or five million to one against you. But someone has to win, and someone does; not you, of course. Let's say it's a fellow fisherman, though, and that he outfits *his* boat with a two-way radio, fifty-caliber machine guns, hand grenades, and a huge bomb which he's going to throw from the flying bridge into the sub's conning tower.

Now, what if you happen to know him? That's possible. The winner has to have friends. And what if he invites *you* to join his crew?

After he has won the million, a lot of people have been attracted to him, some for obvious and not-so-nice reasons. But he has kept his head, or part of it, at least, and he chooses athletes to man his boat: a pair of football players, with the arms of a Sammy Baugh or a Sid Luckman, and the physical attributes necessary to drop the bomb down the sub's hatch. He also chooses a millionaire polo player from Long Island for his mate. (Those millionaires stick together and old money sometimes tolerates new.)

But he doesn't forget his old friends when he picks the crew. He chooses you to work the radio. You don't need to know anything fancy like Morse Code — nothing more difficult than turning a few knobs.

Fortune has smiled upon this man and he is ready to tempt fate again. Sink the heathen Hun. Rid the sea of this savage scourge. Would you join him — join his crew? I hope so, because you'd have fun.

This may sound crazy, but it's no more bizarre than what really happened.

In the summer of 1943, when I was twelve, my father convinced the American Ambassador to Cuba that the forty-foot *Pilar* could be converted into a sub-destroyer, and that she could easily sink one of the German submarines that were preying on Allied shipping in the straits of Florida. By the time Pat and I arrived for the summer, the *Pilar* was armed to the teeth.

Two men were stationed in the bow with submachine guns and two in the stern with BARs and hand grenades. Papa steered on the flying bridge and up there with him was "The Bomb," a huge explosive device, shaped like a coffin, with handles on each end. The idea was to maneuver the *Pilar* next to a sub — how, exactly, wasn't quite clear — whereupon a pair of over-the-hill jai alai players with more guts than brains would heave The Bomb into the open hatch of the conning tower. And then The Bomb would presumably blow the submarine to kingdom come.

As soon as she heard of the scheme, Marty expressed her feelings intelligently, if not dispassionately.

"What if The Bomb misses, Ernest? The conning tower is slightly higher than the bridge of the *Pilar*, and that conning tower is about six feet in diameter while the width of the hatch is only thirty inches across. If the bomb doesn't go down the hatch it won't blow up the sub. It will rattle around until it goes off and blows the conning tower right into you. That will cause some confusion on the sub, of course, but she'll recover and pull away to a thousand yards or so and then her six-inch deck gun will blow the *Pilar* right out of the water."

Marty didn't give papa time to answer. "Kitten, you need a vacation," she continued. "Maybe we could go down the coast to Guanabacoa and you could do that piece you wanted to write on the Chinese watering the human feces they sell to the truck farmers — the one you promised *Collier's* about how the buyers have to sample the stuff with a straw to decide whether it's thick enough."

"Don't you think I know the realities of war?" he said. "I had enough time to contemplate them while the doctors picked those two hundred thirty-seven (or was it two hundred thirty-eight?) pieces of shrapnel out of my leg in the hospital in Milan during World War One."

"Love, this time, if that bomb misses, they won't find two hundred thirty-eight pieces of *you*."

"I know, darling. But the whole project's gone so far now I can't stop it. We have all the equipment on board and signed for, and the crew is terribly excited. Besides, they're all fine men. Neville is not the intellectual type of course — the other day I asked him why he was reading the life of Christ so fast and he said he couldn't wait to see how it ended. But he's basically a good man and loyal, and he fits in perfectly."

"Yes," Marty said, "I think his uncle went down on the *Titanic*."

Papa let that one pass. "Frankly, Hammer, that marine gunner the U.S. naval attaché lent us, is the only one of the crew I have my doubts about. All he does is read comic books. During yesterday's practice run, when we threw the hand grenades at that big green turtle, I called for battle stations and Hammer just said, 'Fuck that. My superior officer said my duties were to operate this here radio and *nothing* else. Why do you think I took this fucking job? I want a rest from the real war. Say, any more of the Scotch left, Ernie? The good Black and White?' "

Papa's imitation of Hammer made them both laugh, Marty a little less loudly, though.

"But I think he's all right," papa said. "He's got combat experience. Maybe he's just had too much war — has battle fatigue or something. Maybe jungle rot, too, from the way his feet smell. You know, that fungus they get in the Pacific. We'll have to get those feet fixed up before we cram nine people . . ."

"Nine? I thought you said seven."

"Well, the boys . . ."

"You're not taking the boys!" Marty screamed.

"Of course not, darling, but they'll be on the boat for the four days' run down to Cayo Confitis, our base island. We'll leave them with Gregorio during the day while we're out on patrol. Of course, if we sight a sub on the way down or back we won't engage it. But I may not let the boys know that. I'll see how they take to the idea of sub-hunting first, and if they aren't frightened it might be great fun and very exciting for them to feel a part of a Q-boat crew."

And it was. My station was in the bow. I was issued my mother's old Mannlicher Schoenauer. She had used it in Africa hunting lions and I felt very proud with it up against my shoulder. But it made a godawful noise and kicked like hell, so I only fired it once.

I'd stay in the bow and practice with a .22, shooting at flying fish which were frightened by the large boat and would take off on incredibly long runs, propelling themselves out of the water with their fins and then gliding for about fifty yards. Sometimes they would flick the water again with their tails and glide for what seemed like an eternity. They were great to practice on because you could see just where your shots were hitting the water, and I learned that even with a rifle, it was necessary to lead a moving target, if the target was far enough away.

The sea was very rough when we left Havana and headed toward the south coast of Cuba and the island of Confitis. The boat was pounding, pounding, pounding into the waves, but when we were about half an hour out the monotony was broken by Gregorio shouting, "Feesh, papa! Feesh!"

Papa jumped down off the flying bridge as the fish knocked the bait out of the outrigger with its bill. Then papa took off the drag from the reel, letting the line run freely, and continued: "One chimpanzee, two chimpanzee, three chimpanzee, four chimpanzee . . ." all the way up to fifteen.

Papa brought in the fish in eighteen minutes flat. It was a marlin, and weighed about 600 pounds.

Gregorio took some fillets and we threw the rest overboard. Within about fifteen minutes he gave another cry. It was a marlin, again. I noticed papa only counted to five before striking the rod after the bait had come out of the outrigger and this fish jumped an awful lot more. He'd propel himself into the air, coming out long and beautiful, then make a series of jumps like a ballet dancer, out of the water, back in, out, back in, in a straight line for three hundred yards or so. It was the longest run of a fish jumping I'd ever seen.

This one was a lot harder to bring in because he was hooked in the mouth, papa not having waited so long to strike him. He finally got the fish in. Then he did something I'd never seen him do before. Papa told Gregorio to release the hook.

"We'll always remember those jumps," papa said. "I'd rather release him and give him his life back and have him enjoy it, than 'immortalize him' in a photograph."

The second day out we saw a whale shark, the largest fish in the sea, sixty feet long, with black and white polka dots on his dorsal side. He was just basking on the surface, docile and harmless. We went right up beside him, and Gregorio poked him in the side with an oar, to see if he could make him move, but it was like poking the side of a building.

"Christ," he said, "that thing's enormous."

"Yes," papa said. "Almost a third the size of the sub we're looking for."

Papa said that this huge fish lives entirely on plankton, a form of minute marine life which it takes in through its mouth and strains like a sieve through some mechanism in its gills. I could see how that is a good way for them to feed as they are so huge that they could never live off other fish if they had to hunt for them.

The following day we saw a school of killer whales. I couldn't express it at the time, but in retrospect they seemed to represent all the evil in nature. But then they just frightened me. Papa said we should give them a wide berth because they had been known to attack fishing boats, breaking them up with their ramrodlike heads and sometimes eating the crew. He said they'd go into a school of tuna and just kill for the fun of it, sometimes not stopping even to eat what they had killed.

They weren't very big for whales, only about eighteen to twenty feet long. But they were built for speed, like porpoises, and they kept moving in synchronization, back and forth, breaking the water together, turning in unison, always moving, always hunting. When I was older I saw wild dogs in Africa which reminded me of these killer whales in the way they, too, were constantly on the move. One knew they had to do a lot of killing and eating to fuel such a frenzied pace.

In the evening we'd pull into shore at some harbor or cove. The first night I was assigned to a berth down below, next to Hammer, and his feet smelled terrible. I almost threw up all over him before I got out of there, but as he was always drunk by six o'clock, the poor bastard probably would not have noticed. When we went up topside for a breather it was really beautiful. The stars seem brighter in those latitudes, especially when you're out on the water, away from pollution. There must have been millions of them, some much, much brighter than others. Pat was interested in astronomy and had told me something about Orion's Belt and other constellations. I tried to pick out the North Star, too, but there were so many stars that I couldn't be sure that I'd found it.

Papa had bought Pat a beautiful telescope, as he always encouraged our interests, but papa himself wasn't really interested in astronomy and would say, never to Pat of course, "Sure, they're up there and they're beautiful and they're a great aid to navigation at night, but to make one's life work studying them seems sort of pointless. How can they help us any more than they already have? Star-gazing is just what the term implies."

The next morning, on the second day out, the country started to get beautiful too. It looked the way the Florida Everglades must have looked in the old days, with colors the hues of a Turner painting, and flocks of flamingos standing in the shallow waters, sometimes rising like undulating pink clouds floating over the early morning mist still covering the water. It was like the dawn of creation and it put papa in a religious mood.

"Can you look at this country and doubt there's a God, Gig?" I knew he didn't expect an answer.

"But I've seen other country, too," he went on. "Perhaps God has his good and bad days . . ."

"I thought you said it was blasphemy to joke about God," I said.

"I joke a lot about organized religion because I don't think Bible pushers have the Word any more than I do. I wouldn't kid Our Lord, for example, if He was on the Cross, but I would try to joke with Him if I ran into Him chasing the money-changers out of the Temple.

"But never joke about a man's religion in front of him," he warned me. "A hell of a lot of people get comfort from their religion. Who knows, they might even be right."

Then we hit bottom.

"Jesus Christ!" Papa immediately stopped all engines, put the *Pilar* in reverse, and backed off slowly, with the screws churning up mud; there was an awful sound as if the boat were human and in agony. Next to us and his wife and his cats, I think my father loved the *Pilar* more than anything on earth and I felt sick as we went around opening all the floorboard coverings to see if water was coming in.

But there weren't any leaks. Papa said there had been a slight mistake in the chart which showed the depth at low tide to be three feet higher than it actually was. Perhaps. Sometimes sand shifts and time obliterates landmarks, but it was also conceivable that papa had made a slight mistake.

We reached Cayo Confitis just before dark. The whole island couldn't have been much larger than the skating rink at Rockefeller Center, maybe 100 yards in diameter. It was flat and unoccupied except for a shack in the center, with a radio antenna on top, and a huge flagpole next to the shack.

Cuba's proud colors were still aloft but at sunset three bored-looking little men marched out in formation from the shack, waved to us, and with great ceremony proceeded to haul down the flag. One man worked the ropes; the officer, identified as such by some rusty braid loosely attached to one shoulder, stood at attention, and the third man stood slightly behind the officer, picking his nose.

It was the sort of post the officer might have been assigned to if he was suspected of having an affair with the commandant's wife — or the other two, of committing petty thievery. The officer always showed his rank by wearing a faded tunic; the soldiers just wore khaki shorts coming apart at the seams.

Papa could see that Pat and I were glum at the prospect of spending two months on the island, and he immediately tried to cheer us up.

"I know it looks bleak, guys, and I am not happy either to be separated from you all day while we are out on patrol. But there are some wonderful reefs for spear fishing around here (involuntary twitch of my facial muscles at the mention of scuba diving) and there are plenty of interesting birds to identify, Pat, and you can shoot the edible ones, Gig, after he has identified them. We'll have fun in the evening, reading and playing cards. You'll see, it won't be so bad."

Next day Pat and I stayed on the island fishing, collecting seashells, and skin diving, while papa went out on patrol. Gregorio, who had five kids, kept us company and in the evening rowed us out to join papa when he returned. Everybody on the *Pilar* was tired but in amazingly good humor. We sat around playing cards. We played for what seemed like thousands of dollars and it was pretty exciting if you had a good hand.

There was surprisingly little drinking at first, partly because the supply of alcohol was low, partly because the crew wanted to be in good shape if they spotted a sub. Papa reached for a book more often than a bottle. He had a bag crammed with detective stories, *War and Peace,* and Fraser's *The Golden Bough.*

We had a pig on the island which we were saving to butcher for a feast. One day while I was goggle fishing I'll be darned if I didn't see him swimming out to sea. He just kept right on going and disappeared over the horizon. There was nothing I could do because the dinghy was on the other side of the island.

Papa couldn't have been more pleasant or a better father on that trip. He was wonderfully cheerful with everyone, and keeping several people cramped in a boat in good humor all the time was no easy trick. He talked about subjects that interested the different crew members. To me it was baseball. One time I got into an argument with Neville about Ty Cobb's lifetime batting average and Neville said, "I bet you a hundred dollars it wasn't as high as three sixty-seven."

And I looked him in the eye and said, "Neville, I wouldn't want to take your money." Papa laughed; he appreciated my generosity.

It was great fun for a while — until Hammer won everybody's money at cards and the books ran out, and until it became apparent that the ocean out there was awfully big and that the chances of spotting a sub on it were pretty small.

The submarines were there all right, we would hear them talking back and forth in German at night, but as none of us could speak German very well, this wasn't much help. And, in any event, we had no triangulation device to pin them down. Subs would almost never surface during the day. Thank God they didn't, or I might still be on that bloody island living off shellfish and watching the Cubans raise and lower that flag.

While we were still at Confitis, we received a message from Naval Intelligence directing us to investigate some large caves on the coast that the German subs were rumored to be using as supply depots. Caves as big as Mammoth in Kentucky and stacked full of fuel and sausages, sauerkraut and Bavarian beer! Maybe even Irish whiskey, papa suggested.

In its wildness, my imagination soon matched that of Naval Intelligence. It might be tricky getting past those sentries with their snarling German shepherds, but a diversionary action, or, if necessary — *if necessary* — a frontal assault would do the trick! And what a coup it would be to deprive the whole wolf pack of its booze.

I knew what beer meant to the morale of a crew. We'd experienced a temporary drought when the supply boat to Confitis was a week late. Hammer had begun trembling on the second day and then started seeing things and we'd had to tie him down, no fun with those feet. And Patche and Ermua, the jai alai players, were mumbling darkly of mutiny, of seizing the helm and heading north by northeast for the nearest bar.

"Courage, lads. With God's help relief will soon come," papa said. And it did, in the form of that radio message. We were just about to storm the hut of the Cubans and seize their homemade still.

"Neville, this is straight from Intelligence, so you know how important it is. You head the reconnaissance team, with Ermua as executive officer, and the boys will go as crew. They'll come in handy if the cave narrows down."

It wasn't hard finding the cave, which seemed to be a local tourist attraction: a small boy gladly took us there. There turned out to be no one guarding the entrance, and we were quickly inside. What a sight confronted us! An enormous underground dome a hundred feet high, with beautiful colored stalactites hanging from the top. It was well lit, with bulbs like Christmas tree lights, and you could see where it narrowed down at the far end into a dark tunnel. That was it! The Germans wouldn't be so stupid as to put their invaluable supplies out in the open. That tunnel must lead to another giant cave where the supplies were.

We all lit flashlights, and headed down the tunnel. It seemed to go on for miles. Ermua cut his hand on a rock and Neville couldn't stop the bleeding, so Ermua had to go back. But the three of us pressed on. I was beginning to poop, we'd been walking and crawling and climbing for what seemed like hours. Then the cave got so narrow that Neville couldn't get his enormous bulk through.

"Go on to the end, boys — if there is one. Good luck, I know you won't quit, you know what it means if we find the depot." We went on, and on, and on, our hands bloody from clutching the sharp rocks. The passage got so narrow that only I could fit through, and finally it just petered out. So this was it. Failure.

But what was that there? A beer bottle, no, three or four, in fact. The bottles were empty, but they were German all right. Schlitz. *They* had been here, and the depot must be at the end of one of the hundred passageways that led off the main tunnel. But we'd never be able to search them all today. So I took the bottles and headed back.

When we reached the *Pilar* it was after dark. "Good work, lads, what did you find?" papa asked. Then he saw the smile on my face — and that I was carrying something. He broke into a broad grin.

"You did it, Gig, you did it! Let me see what you've got."

I handed over the bottles. But when he turned on his flashlight to examine them, his face fell.

"They're German beer bottles, Gig, yes. But made in the States by naturalized Germans. They were probably just left there by picnickers."

I was crying and Neville was practically crying too. Papa turned to him and said, "You gave it your best shot, old man, I'm proud of you. I'm recommending you for the Naval Cross for leading this expedition and also — " he chuckled — "an eventual transfer to Naval Intelligence."

Hammer's feet finally put an end to the trip. The fungus rot got so bad that he couldn't wear shoes anymore and the combined sight and smell of those feet began to elicit pity from all of us, the first pity we'd felt for him since he'd won our money.

Papa, who knew some medicine, was afraid that Hammer's feet might have to be amputated unless he got treatment, so we called off the chase and headed back to Havana. The Cubans showed little emotion when we left. They were beyond that, poor devils.

On the return trip all of us were edgy. The absence of women didn't bother me, and I thought it was stupid the way the others talked of nothing else.

"God, how I miss María," Patche, one of the jai alai players, said. "She really loves me and prays for my safe return every night. She's a saint, that woman. She goes to Mass every Sunday and prays for the soul of her dead mother, too." I'd met María at a party papa gave for the jai alai players, and to me she was obviously a worn-out old whore, with a fat face and heavy thighs. But Patche was hooked. He even mentioned an insurance policy he had taken out, with the money going to María in the event anything happened to him. They "both" thought it the prudent thing to do.

But everything had become distorted and unreal on Cayo Confitis and we were eager to get back home.

Early on the morning of the second day papa sang out from the flying bridge:

"On deck, amigos! Looks like a schooner on a reef."

"Schooner on a reef!" we shouted from below to show we'd heard. Within less than a minute, we were on deck, yawning, tucking in shirt tails, or peeing over the side.

Sleepy as I was, I could still enjoy the orange light slowly emerging and the mist still just above the water. The schooner was anchored on the lee side of a reef. Three small boats alongside were filled with people busy doing something.

Papa looked through his binoculars.

"She's a long way from home," he said. "Let's ease in and see what she's up to. Be fun for the kids to take a look."

Papa must have noticed how groggy I looked.

"Time for a first coffee, eh Gig?" he said. "Run down and get something started in the galley."

By the time I got back topside with the coffee, the gray hull of the schooner had grown to huge proportions. The three dories were away from the mother hull and one of them was loaded with something dark and baffling. Less than a hundred yards away, the schooner's crew lined her rail and one of them hailed us in Spanish.

"Good morning, friends," the man said. "Do you need any fish?"

"We are fishermen, too," papa called back. "Do you need any help?"

"Only if you would like to help us seine this reef."

"Pat, toss them a cockpit line. And you there, a line forward."

In a minute we were alongside and made fast. While Gregorio and papa discussed the seining operation with the captain, the rest of us climbed aboard the big ship and admired her vast amount of deck room. She was the *Margarita* out of Havana and Gregorio knew the skipper's brother.

Suddenly papa cleared his throat loudly, spat over the side, and prepared to address our crew.

"Caballeros — " He grinned as he said that and I figured he must be feeling good from the first gin and tonic of the day to address fishermen as "horsemen."

"We've been invited aboard for breakfast and will then assist the crew with their seining operation. I believe it entails swimming, so nonswimmers will be excused. Patche is excused in any event as he has the best eyes and will serve as lookout for the sub. I've told the captain of the *Margarita* that we're expecting a skiff with supplies and ice and that we have to keep a lookout because the skiff might not see the *Pilar* because of the bulk of the *Margarita*."

Pat and I looked at the ship's massive anchor while papa went to talk to the captain again.

"Boys," papa called. "Come over here and meet Captain Marina. He commands this great vessel and you are his guests. Don't drop any food on deck and leave everything as clean as it is."

We shook hands solemnly with the captain. He smiled, maybe because we were so serious.

"Can we watch while the seine is being set?" Pat asked.

"Watch, hell!" This was the surprise papa had been saving for us. "You can help set it, Pat. The schooner will be our floating base today and if the lookout sights anything we can hurry back to the *Pilar* and try to close with them." (I giggled a little at the mention of the lookout and got a fierce look from papa; he still believed in our mission with the faith of a visionary, and the strength of his pride and belief was perhaps the only thing that maintained discipline among our disheartened crew.)

"Perhaps the *Margarita* will bring us luck," he said, looking at me, eyes blazing.

Seining a reef is a simple operation and one that's been done for thousands of years by every race of fishermen since the Phoenicians. We loaded an extraordinarily long net into three dories and gradually dropped it into the water so that it encircled the reef. Cork buoys kept it afloat on one edge, and lead weights on the other edge held it on the bottom.

Then we began to bring in the net, sometimes standing on the reef, sometimes just hanging onto the net for support. I was tugging on it, diving to free it when it caught on the live coral.

The only thing I worried about was sharks, because we were near the edge of the Gulf Stream again. I was separated from papa most of the day, but when I saw him I asked about sharks.

"You're too ugly. You'd frighten them off, Gig," he said, making light of last summer's scare. Then, seeing that I wasn't reassured, he became serious:

"With all this sunlight they can see the net clearly. It's not part of the usual scenery and a deepwater shark is a very conservative animal. There's danger."

◇ 84 ◇

Toward the end of the day the net had been tightened into a diameter of perhaps eighty yards. We could see what seemed to be almost every fish in the ocean in that enclosure and they were definitely worried now, they knew that something was up, that this was no ordinary day for them.

To scare the fish out of their holes in the coral, we banged on the sides of the dories. Several of the best swimmers from the *Margarita*, holding their breath for an unbelievably long time, dove to the bottom of the enclosed area and spread a smaller net under the fish that had been scared out of the coral. We had them now.

With our heads underwater, Pat and I watched as the seine was gradually lifted. A whole school of jacks moved in unison, up and away. Turtles and small- to medium-sized sharks seemed to come from nowhere. Now all the fish were taking evasive action.

Pat surfaced, too, and swam toward the *Pilar*.

"I want to get my camera for this," he called out. "Ever see so many fish in one place?"

I could easily pick out the circling school of jacks, the compressed groupings of snappers, the pretty reef fish, and the ocean-going pompano. They were jumping high in the air and shivering with terror.

Along with the food fish, we had swept up barracuda, which had shown no more cunning than the others. They, too had been spooked by the approach of that long brown cloud of two-inch mesh that now enclosed them.

"Gig, come over here!"

I ran over to papa. The schooner's crew was dipping out the first of the catch with hoop nets on long poles and carrying their flopping, squirming loads to the hatch. Papa held up a tiny fish, less than six inches long, that had fallen out of a passing net. It had big eyes for its head and an embryonic beak. And yes, a fin that ran all along its back, almost to its tail.

"Beautiful, isn't he?" papa said. "I've never seen one so small. In a few years he would have grown to a seventy-five-pound sailfish. Why don't you take him back to the *Pilar* and put him in one of the specimen jars, Gig? If he's no use to an ichthyologist, I'd love to have the little fellow mounted."

In the next half hour, the bigger, faster fish milled around even more wildly and we lost some that leaped to their freedom. Finally it was time for the last three sharks. They all seemed more than five feet long. No sharks, huh, I kept thinking to myself.

Two crewmen got a hoop net and followed one of the sharks from behind, while another pair of deck hands made a frontal approach with another net. By clever maneuvering they netted the shark at both ends, lifted it onto the deck and, before you could say Moby Dick, a particularly rough looking character had grabbed an ax and severed the shark's spine, just behind the brain. It was too neat, too quick for my taste, like a Mafia execution, but it kept the shark's jaws from snapping off bare feet. The meat was cut into small fillets to be soaked in brine and dried.

Our final big catch of the day was a green turtle that must have weighed eighty pounds. The sharks could have nipped his flippers but were more concerned with escape. One of the crew dived into the floating aquarium and, keeping his hands well away from the sea turtle's head, grabbed the two front flippers. The turtle tried to swim down through the mesh below but the crewman headed him up and when they both surfaced, another crewman grabbed the rear flippers, and a third lashed all four together. They passed him up on deck where he lay helpless on his back.

"Amigos de la mar, you are really serious fishermen," the captain said, approaching us at the rail.

Papa answered him in ceremonial Spanish.

"We were honored to have been present at this demonstration of your technical skill. I had always wanted to learn your methods, and I also thank you for having given my sons valuable instruction. We are at your orders for any further assistance in getting your catch aboard."

Captain Marina was obviously pleased, and spoke again to papa, who grinned and then turned to us.

"We are all invited to dinner, even Hammer, and if we keep him downwind we ought to have a real feast. I'll contribute that ham and throw in some rum."

The feeling of a wonderful sense of communal accomplishment came flooding in on me. Pat and I had worked as crew members on today's catch, and I felt we'd done pretty well.

But what a life the sea was! Maybe it would have paled after a while, but that day was so beautiful and clean and free that I wanted to stay on the *Margarita* forever.

It was one of the happiest days of my life.

Everyone was a little hung over the next morning. It was past seven when the *Pilar* reached open sea, and we were all on the flying bridge when Neville saw it.

"Submarine! Submarine! About ten points off the starboard

bow and closing. Approximate range one thousand yards. She must have just surfaced. I scoured that area a few minutes ago."

"Battle stations," papa said, almost inaudibly. "But take it easy. Normal movements. No rushing. Try to make your faces seem calm. We don't know how powerful their binoculars are."

Once below decks, though, I moved fast, got my Mannlicher Schoenauer from under my bunk and loaded it. Pat was up in the bow, ahead of me, on the starboard side, loading his 303 Lee-Enfield. We grinned at each other, too excited to be afraid. War is a great game for boys.

Hammer murmured, "Fighting's not in my fucking orders!" But he finally limped to his post.

The Bomb was already on the flying bridge and the two jai alai players were unloosening its fastenings.

"Christ," Neville said, staring through his binoculars. "She's as big as a battleship."

"But she doesn't seem to be getting any bigger," papa said, and took the glasses from Neville. After a few seconds he handed the glasses back.

"Neville, it's not closing. It's heading AWAY from us," he said with cold, furious control in his voice. "And not only that. It's PULLING away from us. Our max speed is twelve knots. Hers is a lot more than that. She looks to be about fifteen hundred yards away now."

Then papa laughed and said in Spanish to Patche, "Can you throw The Bomb fifteen hundred yards?"

By now no one needed field glasses to tell that the sub was losing us fast, moving majestically on the dead-calm sea.

Everybody was cursing. Patche yelled, "Come back and fight, you yellow sons of whores!" By now the sub was just a dot on the horizon. We were stunned; the last thing we had expected was to be ignored by the enemy.

In the silence that followed we could hear the radio operator flushing the john.

Later that evening papa told me, "I had decided that we wouldn't close with you and Pat on board." And in a lower voice, "I bet some of the U-boat crew are just kids, too. It's trite to talk about war: Sherman said it all. War is necessary sometimes. Maybe. You wonder."

He was mocking orators now:

"Someone else will fight for me on the beaches. December seven, a day that will live in infamy, will be avenged by younger men. Hell, fix me a gin and tonic, will you, Gig? We're heading home."

Wives

WHEN WE CAME HOME from the sea, Marty thought papa would resume his writing. But he had other plans.

"You're the writer in the family now, Marty," he announced — and he meant it completely and wholeheartedly!

Marty was flattered at first, then amazed, and finally disgusted. To *help* her career was fine, but for America's foremost novelist to retire at forty-four, two years after the completion of *For Whom the Bell Tolls,* was unthinkable — even for a pioneer women's libber like Marty.

I knew it was wrong, crazy even. Was the passive side of papa's personality, a side that we all share, finally getting the upper hand? Or did he feel even then that he had reached his peak, had shot his wad, so to speak, had not surpassed or come close to his idols Tolstoy and Dostoyevsky? Would it be all downhill from now on?

Jesus, he was tired of the lists, tired of competition. Perhaps he was afraid of defending what he called his "title" again. That's human, that's understandable. But nobody would ever let papa just be human.

"They always ask you 'What are you working on now, Ernie?' " he said to me once. "I tell the stupid ones 'the greatest thing since Shakespeare,' and that shuts them up. They believe it, and just smile a sort of 'That's our Ernie' smile. With the intelligent ones it's tougher. If I don't like them, they get a foxy smile and a knowing 'you'll see.' I tell my intelligent friends, and I can count them on the fingers on one hand, that I'm working on a trilogy about the land, the sea, and the air. And I am. But it's not going good. Writing's got to flow and come easy if it's good and this stuff 'smells of the lamp.' You know that old phrase — smells like you've been up all night working on it over a kerosene lamp.

"I may not be going so good, but Marty is writing beautifully. I know so much more about the trade than she does and can help her in so many ways. She has great talent and what she needs is a great editor." He smiled to show that he wasn't really boasting.

"Let's give Marty a chance. She deserves one."

That's how it really was. Marty has always been pictured as an overly ambitious woman who neglected her wifely chores, neglected Ernest, and finally deserted him. That is the official version fed to papa's biographer Carlos Baker through Ernest's after-the-fact letters to his friends. But let's get the facts clear. Marty never deserted him. She was driven from that house in Cuba, driven away by the return in greater force of papa's megalomania. His idea of making Marty the writer in the family was doomed to fail, not because of her lack of talent but because of my father's compulsion to be Number One.

Suddenly he turned on her. "So you don't think I can write anymore," I once heard him say to her. "I'll show you, you conceited bitch. They'll be reading my stuff long after the worms have finished with you." Probably so, but God, what a way to treat someone you loved.

I later learned their breakup wasn't quite so simple. According to papa there was also a basic sexual problem that explained a lot of their arguments. It could have been easily corrected by a visit to a doctor, but my father rarely took the direct approach with his women. He just tortured Marty and when he had finally destroyed all her love for him and she had left him, he claimed she deserted him.

He had used a similar rationalization with my mother, claiming that it was the necessity to practice coitus interruptus that had broken up that marriage. But any fool, and certainly a doctor's son, knew there are some periods of the month when one can have satisfying intercourse without fear of pregnancy.

So when he fell in love with Marty, the whole onus for the breakup of my parents' marriage was placed on my mother's two Caesarean births and the fact that the doctor had told her that she must not become pregnant again. The thing that really made that alibi absurd was papa's often stated belief that too much intercourse was counterproductive to good literature. To put it simplistically, he felt he had to save some of his creative juice for his writing.

Papa would suffer for a long time with a woman who was giving him problems sexually, but in the end he would make her suffer more.

During the late 1930s, he used to cuckold Mother unmercifully in Havana with an American lady friend — he screwed so many times that it's a wonder he had anything left for Mother at all. Once he almost broke his toe jumping out of a hotel window when Mother arrived at the place unexpectedly.

Damn. All those wives. Mother got it right when she said, "I don't mind Ernest falling in love but why does he always have to marry the girl when he does?"

He would feel himself beginning to stagnate after he had been married to one wife for a while. I think most men feel that way but it's more frightening for creative artists than most, because their very being depends on inspiration and they need new and stimulating experiences to fire their productive motors.

The trouble is that most people can't justify the continued emotional ravaging of others. Papa was no exception. The periodic injection of high-octane creative energy left more of a hangover of contrition and remorse each time, as there were more bodies left behind after each divorce. But something kept justifying his actions, whispering in his ear, "You're beyond the law. The law only applies to ordinary mortals."

Women, some women anyway, do not enter into marriage for a casual ride down the road. When they marry, it's their one big trip, especially if there are children, and if you stop and let them off, it takes something out of you to look back at your wife and your children by the side of the road and see that dazed look on their faces.

So you don't look back, except in your sleep when you can't help it. But somehow your sleep isn't quite as restful, and while you're awake, you just drive faster to keep your mind off those eyes.

Papa went to Europe in 1944, and had his taste of war at last. When he returned, he was like many servicemen coming back to those who loved them — uncomprehensible but treated with loving solicitude by relatives who could only imagine what they had experienced. Hyperactive, incessantly talking of war and about people who had fought with him, calling them by their names without bothering to identify them, as if we, too, knew them intimately. Giving us souvenirs — presented me with a P-38 Walther pistol which he said he'd taken off a dead German captain. ("Shot the bastard myself, Gig.")

Telling stories far into the night. How it was at Rambouillet, when he'd led his "army" of several hundred French Maquis into Paris ahead of everybody, beating General Leclerc by a good twenty-four hours. How he'd been put in for the Silver Star by another general, who was grateful for the intelligence he had supplied on the enemy's position; but then how he had to solemnly deny his activities before a court of inquiry when it was discovered, rather belatedly by that same officer, that correspondents weren't allowed to carry arms under the terms of the Geneva Convention. (Other correspondents, perhaps because they had been scooped, resented his one-man war and contributed to that court of inquiry.)

He'd had a severe concussion, having hit a water tower while driving through the London blackout with no lights, and for the first time, too, pidgin English dominated his way of speaking, as if all personal pronouns had become battle casualties. His speech was punctuated by, "How do you like it, now, gentlemen?" said over and over to no one in particular and described so graphically by Lillian Ross in her *New Yorker* profile, a piece of work which was unintentionally devastating because it showed him *exactly* as he was at that time.

A new and wonderful girl was coming soon to take Marty's place at the Finca. "She's truly beautiful, Gig, you'll love her." I knew I must and probably would. But I thought of Mother's words — why does he always have to marry when he falls in love?

We had all been worked into a frenzy over his anticipation of the arrival of his new wife-to-be; and oddly enough she wasn't a disappointment. If anything, she was prettier than Marty, and even more fun for us children because we were older and could share so many more things with her.

Mary Welch was a small, almost petite, blonde who had been a war correspondent for *Time* magazine in London. Papa had met her during his breakup with Marty, so there had been the usual relatively comfortable transition for him: a lovely woman available while he was in the process of killing the memories of the last. And Mary was easy to kill memories with.

Unlike some women who only pretend to share their husband's interests during their courtship, Mary shared them afterwards as well. She'd go fishing day after day on the *Pilar*, before and after their marriage, exposing her fair Nordic skin to the tropical sun without complaint. Mary also learned Spanish quickly and well. She had a good ear for pronunciation and the self-discipline to study the grammar, too. And she brought order to the domestic chaos that Marty had left behind.

Papa could never bring himself to fire a servant. The original ones that Marty had hired were still there and, by the time of Mary's arrival, firmly entrenched. She got the gardener, a cockfighting devotee who drank too much, to show up for work at least three days a week, and within six months one could see the outline of the house again. But Clara, the psychotic maid, attacked the Chinese cook with a butcher knife and it became apparent that she had to go. Not long afterward the same cook, who during Marty's benign and casual reign had frequently come in from the kitchen and announced to guests assembled at the table, "No lunch today," did it one final time and then padded back into his domain and hanged himself from a rusty pipe.

I wasn't there when the suicide occurred but I didn't mourn him for long. Mary, a quick student, had mastered cooking by the time I next returned to the Finca.

She could do everything expected of a woman, but I didn't like her at first despite her accomplishments because she had displaced my true love, Marty. But Mary was sexy too and my period of mourning for Marty didn't last long.

I was fifteen when Mary took over the Cuban house and I remember getting more than the usual professional instructor's pleasure from teaching her to shoot. She learned fast, never flinching at the kick of a twenty-gauge shotgun, which must have been unpleasant for a woman who weighed barely one hundred pounds. It was great positioning her trim body so that the weight was on her front foot and snuggling the gun up comfortably against her shoulder. And I'd put my cheek against hers, just for a second, to make sure that she was lining up the gun sights correctly.

And I felt then that she had a crush on me, too. I remember the time we took the *Pilar* to Puerto Escondido, a wonderfully cool inlet a few miles east down the Cuban coast, where we'd sometimes go to escape the hot summer nights.

On that trip I piloted the *Tin Kid,* a twenty-foot auxiliary craft that papa had bought for Mary, keeping it about forty yards on the toe of the *Pilar,* and to her starboard. It was a pretty rough passage, at least for the smaller *Tin Kid,* and as I stood stoically at the helm, taking a lot of punishment pounding into the easterly blow, I imagined I saw Mary out of the corner of my eye, glancing admiringly over at my not entirely unintentionally noble posture. I hadn't watched papa steering all those years for nothing.

After we reached Puerto Escondido, ate the evening meal, and had quite a few drinks, papa drinking the most, of course, but with Mary and I not far behind, Mary said, "I want to sleep with Mr. Gig tonight."

She said it so sweetly and in such a tone of relaxed admiration that I didn't say a thing, but just took it as my due. Papa, who was getting pleasantly drunk, just said, "Sure, sure, sleep with Mr. Gig."

I thought that was the end of it, but a little later Mary again said, "I want to sleep with Mr. Gig tonight." She repeated it several times in the next few minutes and finally, perhaps a little more defiantly, "Dammit, I'm going to sleep with Mr. Gig tonight."

"Okay, sure, sleep with Mr. Gig," papa said. Fine. Settled. But where, where could we sleep? I was suddenly cold sober. I was going to sleep with Mary and I was one spooked boy.

"Where would we have the most room, papa?" I asked.

"Take the air mattress up on the flying bridge and be sure to take at least two blankets. It will be cold up there before morning."

I made all the arrangements. Blew up the mattress as fast as I could, stopping only twice to catch my breath, tucked in the blankets, got into my pajamas and waited, not really knowing what was expected of me and not having the faintest idea what to do if anything was.

Then I remembered the one thing papa had ever told me

about sex: "The key to making a woman happy in bed is so simple, Gig. They have a thing down there about a third the size of your little finger. It's called the clitoris. It's right in the middle. If you want to make a woman happy, really happy, not just satisfy yourself, first stroke it gently, over and over, like you're petting a cat, ever so gently. (He was stroking our cat Boise under the chin and Boise was purring ecstatically.) It's a woman's sexual trigger, sort of a miniature penis. And if you don't know about it you might as well forget about pleasing women in bed."

But where "down there" was it and "in the middle" of what? Christ!

It seemed as if Mary would never come up. Maybe the whole thing had been called off? I lay on my back, on the far left side of the mattress, my whole body rigid. The wind had died down and the sky had cleared and the stars were out in countless numbers and shone with incredible intensity.

I was trying to find the North Star, with the Little Dipper as a reference point, when my erection slipped from between my legs and made my half of the blankets look like a goddamn tent.

I rolled over on my stomach just as Mary's head appeared over the top of the boat.

"Are you there, Gig?" and seeing me, "Oh, it's a beautiful night. Have you ever seen the stars so clearly before?"

"No, I haven't," I said, faking a yawn.

Thank God the mattress was wide enough so we didn't touch when she got under the covers.

"Look, there's Orion's Belt and the Little Dipper," she said. "And there, that little one which usually looks so much larger is the North Star. It's dwarfed by all the magnificent constellations. There seem to be some out tonight that have never ever been there before. And the light we are seeing from them now started on its way here millions of years ago. Millions, Gig. Isn't that incredible?"

"It sure is," I said, yawning again.

"Oh, you poor darling, you must be dead. All those beers on top of the rough trip down." She turned and touched my shoulder. "Let's go to sleep and hope papa gets a big one in the morning."

And she rolled over and I could tell by the rhythm of her breathing that she was fast asleep in a few moments.

But there was no sleep of the innocent for me. I was terrified that if I fell asleep I'd inadvertently roll over and put my arm around her or do God knows what else. So I rolled over on my back — at least that bloody tent had collapsed — and started identifying constellations. When I tired of that I slipped stealthily out of our bed and went below and had a couple more beers.

But when I went back to topside and crawled in next to Mary I still couldn't sleep. Finally I collapsed from exhaustion around four a.m., repeating over and over to myself, "Stay above Orion's Belt."

I never could remember my dreams the way papa could, but I guess I kept my hands where they belonged because I do remember being gently nudged by Mary around seven, and her saying, "Better get up, Gig. We'll be having breakfast and getting under way soon." And then, "It's a lovely morning. I feel so alive after a good night's sleep down here. You're an excellent sleeping companion, Mr. Gig. You didn't make a sound all night."

Lessons

AT FIFTY PAPA HAD BECOME a snob and a phony. Everything was "Gritti Palace this . . . Cortina that . . . Count So-and-So is really so nice, you'll love him, Gig." Count So-and-So usually turned out to be a no-count nothing.

"And the girl, Gig, she's really something."

Well, she was dull, and had a hook-nosed mother in constant attendance.

These were my introductions to "The Beautiful People."

Papa had joined the international set, and I felt I'd lost him. "I've had a wonderful life, Gig. Never been ashamed of anything I've done. Don't we have fun, Gig? Don't we, god damn it? That's an order, Gig — we have a wonderful life."

Oh shit. I wanted out. But where could I go? It's fine to be under the influence of a dominating personality as long as he's healthy, but when he gets dry rot of the soul, how do you bring yourself to tell him he stinks?

"Don't we have fun, Gig? Don't we . . . "

I was eighteen, and papa was paying for my food, lodging, and schooling. There were still times when we could talk and, strangely, papa could still give good advice. I was in my last year of prep school, thinking about college, and about what would come next.

"It doesn't really matter what you do as long as you do something that really interests you, Gig," he said. "Something that you think is worthwhile and productive. And a lot of things are worthwhile, even though some narrow-minded bastards will say otherwise. And don't worry about money — if you're a failure at birdwatching, I'll support you! Have you thought much about what you'd really like to do?"

Actually, I had thought a lot. I'd had good grades in prep school, could get into almost any college I wanted to, and had the brains for law or medicine. But I hated most lawyers, thought they were sharpies and crooks, while medicine seemed too dull, too staid. What I really wanted to be was a Hemingway hero.

But what the hell was a Hemingway hero? I could analyze all his novels, but by far the simplest explanation was that a Hemingway hero was Hemingway himself, or the better parts of him. Still, to support yourself while doing all the exciting things that allowed you to exhibit grace under pressure, you had to be able to write about them. The passport to this glamorous life was talent, which was God-given, and a knowledge of the mechanics of writing, which could be taught. I decided to become a writer. I make light of it now but I was dead serious then.

"Papa, what books influenced you most when you were a boy?" I asked him one vacation in Havana.

Papa seemed delighted by my question. He gave me a list of books to read, and my apprenticeship began.

Madame Bovary had the simplicity of everything truly beautiful. *War and Peace* was magnificent torture. As papa warned me, it was hard keeping track of the characters with similar names. "But read them for insight into character, organization of plot — and, of course, for fun," he advised.

"Most of the new guys like James Jones and Irwin Shaw have only one good book in them. They can't go the distance, but like good club fighters, they'll grab you, spin you around, distort your vision with their thumb in your eye. They'll hang on, they'll rest against the ropes and live off their one-book reputation for the rest of their lives. Watch their real stinkers that follow. But read *From Here to Eternity* and *The Young Lions* — and of course read Faulkner.

"He's the best of us all — although he can't finish his novels and you have to wade through a lot of crap to get to his gold."

When papa heard that Faulkner had won the Nobel Prize for literature, he said, "Faulkner deserves it; it's just that he lacks a literary conscience. If no nation can exist half slave and half free, you'd think no man could write half whore and half straight. But Faulkner can. God, I'd love to have his talent."

After a few more whiskeys, papa said, "I'll settle just for being his manager, like Leo Durocher, who never had the tools to play baseball, is happy now just to manage Willie Mays, who does."

On another night, papa became nostalgic about friends who had shared his moveable feast, in Paris during the 1920s. "Ezra Pound — most generous friend I ever had. Even convinced myself he was crazy when insanity was his only defense against treason. Axis Sally was sentenced to twenty years for broadcasting enemy propaganda and Lord Haw-Haw was hanged. That was uppermost in our minds when a group of us tried to get the treason charge dropped — and we succeeded — so poor Ez was committed to St. Elizabeth's Hospital in Washington."

"Was he a traitor?"

"He was in Italy when war broke out. The people flattered his ego — put a microphone in front of him so thousands could hear his voice. Ez loved to talk and did so brilliantly. But he wasn't crazy. Just talked too much. Sure, he had some nutty economic ideas, but so does the average Joe who goes to Vegas."

Papa rarely forgot Scott Fitzgerald when we had these talks. "*Gatsby* was a great book. I've read it twice in the last five years. It gets better with each reading. *Tender Is the Night* is a fine book, too. Flawed in the middle. But so is my *To Have and Have Not*. *This Side of Paradise* is a joke, though. And *The Beautiful and the Damned* is so damned unbeautiful I couldn't finish it! Scott's writing got better and better, but no one realized it, not even Scott. Despite his rummyhood and perhaps *because* of Zelda, who really made him the box with the handles, he got better and better. The stuff he was writing at the end was the best of all. Poor bastard."

It wasn't true that papa didn't have a good word for his contemporaries, especially the up-and-coming ones. But it was true that he gave them mixed reviews.

"Mailer's probably the best postwar writer. He's a psycho, but the psycho part is the most interesting thing about him. Chances are he won't be able to throw another fit like *The Naked and the Dead*. But if he does," papa said, throwing a punch at an imaginary Mailer, "I better watch out. There'll be another Dostoyevsky to contend with and no one lasted more than three rounds with Mr. Dostoyevsky."

I suppose papa was talking more to himself than to me the

evening he said, "I've figured the Nobel Prize out. It's those bloody literal-minded Swedes, or, if you prefer, those honest, faithful Swedes.

"According to the terms of Nobel's will, it must go to fiction of redeeming social significance. But Gide got it, and there wasn't much uplifting about him . . . Henry James didn't get it, nor James Joyce . . . Poor Wilde never had a chance, with young what'shisname holding his hand. Dreiser, with that boring *American Tragedy*, was actually *considered* because he continually sang of motives so lofty you needed an oxygen mask to read him and Benzedrine to stay awake . . . They gave it to Sinclair Lewis. Maybe they thought anyone with a face like that must have suffered and therefore have become noble and uplifting . . . I bet Aimee Semple McPherson made the short list that year! But Pearl Buck! *The Good Earth* maybe, but Jesus, the awful stuff that followed! She's a fine lady but I'll be glad when she gets a spadeful of good earth in her face. No, I won't really . . . But it's fun to talk about these 'great' writers."

That summer in Havana I read papa's favorites, from *Huckleberry Finn* to *Portrait of the Artist as a Young Man:* like him, I sometimes had two or three books going at the same time. Then papa steered me to the short story masters, Maupassant and Chekhov. "Don't try to analyze — just relax and enjoy them."

"Now," papa said one morning. "Try writing a short story yourself. And don't expect it to be any good."

I sat down at a table with one of papa's fine-pointed pencils and thought and thought. I looked out of the window, and listened to the birds, to a cat crying to join them; and to the scratch of my pencil, doodling. I let the cat out. Another wanted in.

I went to papa's typewriter. He'd finished with it for the day. Slowly I typed out a story and then took it to him.

Papa put his glasses on, poured himself another drink, and read, as I waited. He finished it and looked up at me. "It's excellent, Gig. Much better than anything I could do at your age. Only change I'd make is here," and he pointed to the line about a bird falling from its nest and finding, miraculously, that if it flapped its wings, it wouldn't crash on the rocks below.

"You've written . . . 'All of a sudden he realized he could fly.' Change 'all of a sudden' to 'suddenly.' Never use more words than you have to — it detracts from the flow of action." Papa smiled. I hadn't seen him smile at me like that for a long time. "But you've won the lottery, pal. Writing takes study, discipline, and imagination. You've shown me with this that you have the imagination. And if you can do it once, you can do it a thousand times. Imagination doesn't leave you for a long time, maybe never. Dostoyevsky was fifty-seven when he wrote *Crime and Punishment*.

"God, I used to get sad in Key West when people sent me their work and I could tell after reading one page that they didn't have it and never would. I answered every goddamn letter, usually saying that writing well was mainly a matter of luck, that to be given a great talent was like winning a million-to-one lottery; and if you weren't blessed, all the study and self-discipline in the world wouldn't mean a thing. If their letter had something like 'Everybody says I'd make a great engineer but what I really want to do is write,' I'd answer, 'Maybe everybody isn't wrong and you'll probably make an excellent engineer and then forget all about writing and be delighted you never went into it.'

"I wrote hundreds of letters like that and I was getting a dollar a word in those days.

"Later, when there were even more letters, I shortened my answers to 'Writing is a tough trade. Don't get mixed up in it if you can help it.' They probably thought, 'That conceited son of a bitch probably hasn't even read my stuff. But because he can write, he makes a big exclusive thing of it.'

"The important thing is, Gig, that now I can teach *you* because you have the tools. And, in all immodesty, I know a lot about the trade.

"I've wanted to cut down for a long time. The writing doesn't come so easily for me anymore. But I'll be just as happy helping you as doing it myself. Let's have a drink to celebrate."

Only once before can I remember papa being as pleased with me — when I tied for the pigeon-shooting championship. And he was confident that there was another winner in the family when I entered the short story for a school competition and won first prize.

Turgenev should have won the prize. He wrote the story. I merely copied it, changing the setting and the names, from a book I assumed papa hadn't read because some of the pages were still stuck together.

I didn't feel like a winner and wondered how long it would be before papa found out that the only creative contribution I had made to the story was to alter "suddenly" to "all of a sudden."

Fortunately I wasn't around when papa discovered my plagiarism. It got back to me that someone asked him if his son

Gregory wrote. "Yes," he replied, with gusto and sparkle, flashing that "say cheese" smile he sometimes affected. "Gregory writes an occasional bad check." And, of course, everyone laughed.

Someone in that crowd might have thought, "What a brutal bastard to make such a callous wisecrack about his son. I guess all those stories I've heard about him being a hard-shell bully are true."

Hard-shelled, yes, but I helped make that shell.

The Muse

THE NEXT TO LAST TIME I saw my father was during the Christmas holidays in 1950 and he really looked wonderful. His eyes, which had been sad-kind a lot of the time since the early summers of the forties, sparkled again. He had lost weight, too, a sure sign that he wasn't drinking too much and was taking his work seriously. His face was full by then and he'd lost the movie star handsomeness for good, but he'd never been really vain about his looks.

His image was another matter. He'd whip off his glasses the moment he spotted a camera, because he wanted to look tough, nonliterary, and nonintellectual. And, much later, when death was stalking him, he wanted to look young and would comb his hair forward like a Roman senator to hide his baldness. But he seemed to know that his looks were another gift, if on a lower order than his talent, and he'd be damned if he'd take advantage of it. I was always proud of him for that.

He was "in training" again that Christmas, there was no doubt about it, and the reason soon appeared, walked through the front door from the guest house, as a matter of fact. Her name was Adriana Ivancich, and she was a nineteen-year-old Italian noblewoman, whose family Mary and papa had met in Venice two years before. Adriana was an attractive girl with dark hair and eyes, high cheekbones, a thin but not too angular face, and a lovely smile that betrayed no conceit or over-awareness of her lineage. She didn't look at all like my conception of an Italian, which had been formed mostly by contacts with immigrants from southern Italy. In short, she merited papa's basic accolade: she had class.

The Ivanciches had shown the delightful hospitality for which the Italians are so deservedly noted and the Hemingways were ostensibly reciprocating in kind. But it was more than that — much, much more. Papa had fallen in love with Adriana. He had written *Across the River* about her and it hadn't been well received; he was about to launch his final literary voyage with her image as the figurehead of his floundering creative ship.

Now that Adriana was at the Finca, a house guest, relentlessly chaperoned by her mother, papa was ecstatic just to have her nearby. Not to touch, not to kiss, not to make love with. What did Mary think about this? I don't know. I never asked her.

"Gig, I think I've got another shot at the title. I don't want to talk about what I'm writing yet," Papa said, knocking on wood, "but I'm well into it and I'll show it to you as soon as I'm finished. You know how it is, writer." My plagiarism hadn't been discovered yet.

"God, I'm glad, papa. Can't I see just a little of it?"

"No, but I can give you an outline. I've started something on the old Bimini days and it's got you kids in it. I've never used any of the family in print before, except the women — Hadley, your mother, and Marty. Wait and buy the book — it's pretty flattering to you," he kidded.

"What I'm working on now is part of that trilogy I told you about on the land, the sea, and the air. I'm just about finished with the Bimini part, and I'll show you the second section of the trilogy as soon as I finish it, which shouldn't be long at the rate I'm going now. I'd like your reaction on that one. It's different from anything I've written before. No love interest, no sex, just a simple story about an old man catching a fish. It's kind of mystical, though, and the prose is Homeric, maybe too Homeric, like I'm reaching for greatness. But I'm not. It's coming out naturally. Old Bunny Wilson will call it another Hemingway fish story, I guess. But I can always count on John O'Hara to call it the greatest thing since the Sermon on the Mount.

"Remember when John came out with that laudatory review of *Across the River*, saying I was the best writer since Shakespeare, and Hirschfeld had a wonderful cartoon in the *New York Times* showing all the great writers since the Bard impaled on my pen? O'Hara is something. Sometimes the Irish are so loyal they lose all judgment.

"Ever since I told John how good *Appointment in Samarra* was, and he knew I meant it, he's been like a faithful retriever. Next time I see him I'll tell him that *Appointment*'s as good as anything I've ever written — which, by the way, it may be. Perhaps he'll have a stroke and we'll lose a potential future source of embarrassment.

"And on this fish story, we can get Lillian Ross, on a day when the wind's right and the smell's not too bad for her, to do another deadpan piece on me chopping up sharks in the shark factory across the bay, mumbling in incoherent Spanish that it's an end all critics deserve. The critics are bound to read symbolism into the sharks. But I'm breaking the rules and talking too much about this book now. You'll be the first to see it if you're still here, Gig. It's just that I feel so good writing it that I'm mouthing off a bit — maybe that's why I'm so confident about this second part about the old man. It's fun to write again. No more two-finger exercises to keep the typewriter keys from rusting and the mind from atrophying.

"Maybe Man really will prevail, like old corn-drinking Mellifluous said in his Nobel acceptance speech.

"God, I feel strong and I don't think I even need to sleep, but Adriana is so lovely to dream of, and when I wake I'm stronger than the day before and the words pour out of me. They come so fast I can't keep up with them and I don't want to stop, but I force myself to, after five hours, because I know I must be getting tired. When you're tired the words may seem good but all you do is to end up cutting them the next morning.

"But the juices are flowing again, pal. No, not the seminal juices, you lecherous little bastard — " he smiled, catching my grin — "the creative ones.

"I lost the title with *Across the River*. It wasn't as bad as the critics said. But the readers didn't want a romantic novelist writing about getting old and dying and having a narcissistic affair with a young girl. Narcissism — you know what that means — glorying in the image of oneself. Women do it all the time and it's *de rigueur* for them. But it looks foolish and shallow in the middle-aged, even in women."

"You're not middle-aged," I said.

"Technically I am, Gig. Christ, I feel like a young stallion, though. Have you seen her yet?"

"Yes, a few moments ago in the living room. She looked like she's having a good time. But it's a shame her sister Aftera didn't want to come to Cuba."

"In matters of taste there is no dispute," he said, answering my question elliptically, as he knew I preferred Aftera, whom I'd met the previous year in Venice.

"I think you're missing a lot in Adriana, Gig. She doesn't talk much, but she's an intellectual counter-puncher, understands what you're saying and then throws it back at you in a gently mocking way.

"Here they are." He interrupted himself as Adriana and her mother came into the room and he sprang from his chair and offered it to the old baroness. He said something to her in Italian which seemed to please her and then turned to Adriana and shyly offered her a drink.

After he'd made the drink, he took a chair across from her and in a low, confidential voice asked her in English, perhaps for my benefit, how she'd liked her breakfast that morning, if the pool was properly cleaned of the leaves that always fell in it overnight, and if her mother had enjoyed their constitutional around the grounds. Then she smiled and said something I couldn't hear and they both laughed aloud and the baroness's head turned ever so slightly toward them, not startled or alarmed, like a bored sentry protecting an impregnable castle.

And papa and Adriana went on chatting, sometimes in Italian, sometimes in English, and it was nothing really, except that you could tell he was in love, and perhaps the girl was flattered by his attention, or perhaps bored and just being polite or amused, as only young girls can be amused with an infatuated old man, but certainly not in love with him. But very sweet and considerate and never betraying her inner emotions. Never hurting him.

That's the way I like to remember papa.

Across the River

WHEN PAPA CRACKED UP in the fall of 1960 in Sun Valley, nobody but Mary and, of course, the doctor and a few local friends knew about it. He wrote me from the Mayo Clinic that he had hemachromatosis, a rare and eventually fatal form of diabetes. I don't know where he found out about that disease; he was awfully clever about things like that. Maybe he thought that because I was a medical student I required a more sophisticated explanation of his hospitalization than the official story that had been put out about his being treated for high blood pressure.

One thing is clear. The Mayo doctors made a mistake in discharging him when they did. Mary fought like a tigress against his release, pleading for a transfer to a sort of halfway house for the mentally ill, the Institute for Living in Hartford, Connecticut. But the Mayo doctors, the best and the brightest, would have none of this. What was one woman's intuition compared with all that medical expertise?

But the doctors were wrong and they would be the first to

admit it. In all the hospitals I've trained in, some pretty good ones, too, cerebral tissue splattered all over the walls a week after a patient is discharged doesn't constitute a therapeutic triumph.

That my father would tell me the truth about his mental illness was unthinkable. Something physical, sure. But mental, never. He was too much my father, my model, a whole generation's model, and he thought he'd fail those whom he had wanted so desperately to teach, had tried all his life to teach. He'd let us down if he went crazy. They said it was his machismo. I think it deserves a nobler word. His act of deception was as much one of love as it was of pride.

Let's just mention my next-to-last contact with what was left of him, in April 1961, when the money he was sending for my medical school education stopped. The support checks hadn't arrived for two months and I called the Mayo Clinic. I put in a person-to-person call but was connected instead with a doctor who didn't even bother to identify himself. I'll never forget what he said, delivered in that emotionless voice only the greatest of physicians eventually master.

"Maybe your father can't remember getting your letters."

"What do you mean he can't *remember* getting my letters? My father has one of the best memories in the world." No answer from the doctor.

"What do you mean he doesn't remember?" I almost shouted.

"Just that. Maybe he doesn't *remember* getting your letters." His tone was almost hostile now.

"What's your specialty?"

"I'm a psychiatrist."

"Is my father being treated for a mental illness?"

"I'm sorry. I'm not at liberty to disclose the nature of your father's illness." For the first time his voice showed some feeling. "But I'll see what I can do about getting the money sent to you."

"Thanks."

"You're welcome. Goodbye."

I flew out to Sun Valley for his funeral. In the small plane that made the final leg of the journey, my father's older sister, Marcelline, was in the seat next to me. We didn't talk much, which I would have been relieved to do, because Marcelline was too busy taking notes on the other people in the plane, notes that might prove useful for her forthcoming book on Ernest. She had a serious look on her face, almost evangelical, as if she finally believed that he might amount to something.

Mary received us at papa's home — Fort Hemingway, as I immediately christened it. It had been purchased early in his illness, but seemed to presage it. Set well back from the road, it was an almost bunkerlike blockhouse, built of poured concrete to last two hundred years, an ideal buttress against the world, and as safe a refuge as could be found for a paranoid. It lacked only catwalks and an electrified fence to be as secure as Trotsky's redoubt in Mexico.

Mary had been through hell the last two days, starting with the discovery of my father's body. She received us lovingly, in spite of the length of time some of us had been estranged from papa — and the feeling that we had abandoned him, leaving her to stand alone as his final protector. She went out of her way to help arrange our lodging with her friends in the town. The courage and the real class that she showed was the kind one later admired in Mrs. Kennedy, walking down broad Pennsylvania Avenue on that Day of Drums.

The day before the funeral was strange. Hundreds of telegrams of condolence came in from all over the world, but only a small number of people actually showed up. There weren't too many really good friends left. A few from the old days, like Charles Sweeney, the legendary French Foreign Legion Colonel who had fought in seven wars and was one of those rare people of whom it truthfully can be said that he feared no man. (That eighty-year-old gentleman, slightly deaf, gave me some anxious moments in a bar when he discussed foreign affairs in a voice the whole place could hear, accusing Eisenhower of being an incompetent fool and General MacArthur of megalomania. A few rough-looking rednecks turned our way before I could get him the hell out of there.)

And dear, sensitive Charles Thompson, who had hunted with papa in the thirties, and to whom he had dedicated *Green Hills of Africa*. And of course, the hangers-on from Havana, Key West, and Sun Valley — those who had enjoyed the periphery of greatness because they knew that was the closest they would ever come to it. They were a mixed bag, and reminded me of that famous photograph of the corpse of the matador Joselito, lying in a Madrid infirmary surrounded by about thirty intimates, all but two of whom seem more concerned with their appearance in front of the camera than with their friend's death.

My brother Pat flew in from Africa, and he and Jack and I were all together for the first time since the late forties, when we'd spent a wonderful summer fishing in Idaho, Wyoming, and Montana. Although we three were properly solemn at first, we soon found ourselves laughing and joking together as we had in the old days. I was vaguely ashamed, feeling that we should be spending most of the time thinking about papa and going over the wonderful times we'd had with him. But the three of us were irrepressible, and discussed almost nothing but our own plans. I had the damndest feeling that now I really would become a doctor.

One other unlikely thing happened during that time before we buried papa. I was staying with Clara Speigel, an old friend of his, and she had generously let me use her station wagon while I was in town. While driving from Ketchum toward Sun Valley, I saw a tall young girl in bluejeans walking by the side of the road. I offered her a lift and was surprised when she accepted. She was Irish, had their lovely complexion, and wonderful amber green eyes that changed color while you watched.

Her name was Valery Danby-Smith and she had been my father's secretary for a year, until about ten months before his death. She was now working as a researcher for *Newsweek*. She wasn't out there on an assignment and the trip to Sun Valley had been expensive. But she said she'd had to make it. I liked her right from the start and I finally fell in love with her and we were married in 1966.

Then it was finally time for what we had come for. I confess I felt profound relief when they lowered my father's body into the ground and I realized that he was really dead, that I couldn't disappoint him, couldn't hurt him anymore.

He had chosen nothingness, semi-voluntarily, and now we were giving him a semi-Christian burial, omitting some of the service as is required for those who still have an option. Sometimes madness can be more frightening than death. Papa had never been afraid of much and I respected his decision.

The priest's mind was elsewhere. He had been instructed to read from Ecclesiastes, which papa knew put men in their proper place: "One generation cometh and another passeth away, but the land abideth forever." But he stopped short of the phrase, "The Sun Also Rises . . ."

Then I thought, I hope it's peaceful, finally. But, oh God, I knew there was no peace after death. If only it were different, because nobody ever dreamed of, or longed for, or experienced, less peace than he. He wrote of that longing all his life, in words as simple and as complicated as autumn and as spring.

If only he could still dream somewhere. He loved to dream. He longed to be of the land and the sea and the sky and at least now he was a part of them.

"Atoms can't dream, Gig," I could hear him say. "No use deluding yourself, old pal."

There was no solace in thinking of clichés, even that wonderful one about how it would be a long time before the world would see his like.

I would never see him again.